School Struggles

School Struggles

A Guide to Your
Shut Down Learner's Success

Richard Selznick, PhD

SENTIENT PUBLICATIONS

First Sentient Publications edition 2012
Copyright © 2012 by Richard Selznick, PhD

A paperback original

Cover design by Kim Johansen, Black Dog Design, www.blackdogdesign.com
Book design by Timm Bryson

Library of Congress Cataloging-in-Publication Data
 Selznick, Richard.
 School struggles : a guide to your shut down learner's success / Richard Selznick.
   p. cm.
 ISBN 978-1-59181-178-7
 1. Reading--Remedial teaching. 2. Education--Parent participation. 3. School failure--Prevention. I. Title.
 LB1050.5.S37 2012
 372.43—dc23
                                    2012017967

Printed in the United States of America

10 9 8 7 6 5 4 3 2 1

SENTIENT PUBLICATIONS
A Limited Liability Company
www.sentientpublications.com

School Struggles is dedicated to my wife,

GAIL

for everything—patience, understanding,
love and…all the great meals.

Also, to my children,

JULIA & DANIEL

for making it all worthwhile.

Contents

— — — — — —

PART TWO
STRUGGLING ON THE SCHOOL ROAD (ADHD AND OTHER RELATED ISSUES) 67

Acknowledgments

—— —— —— —— —— ——

I would like to thank my friends, family and colleagues for all of the encouragement and support in the writing of this book. Thanks, as well, to the staff and families of the Cooper Learning Center and the Department of Pediatrics of the Children's Regional Hospital/Cooper University Hospital.

A note of appreciation goes to Janice Culley, Rabbi Gerri Neuberg, Dr. Andrea Fina, Pat Gerke, and Susan Chavis (yes, you're in the book) for preliminary readings of *School Struggles* and all of your commentary. Thanks, as well, to Dr. John Kellmayer for ongoing counsel and support. Thanks to Patrick Flanigan for the video production and filming of the Logan School/Shut-Down Learner project and other photography for *School Struggles*.

I would like to extend my appreciation to Helen Townsend, my "west coast editor," who helped to bring this book into shape. Helen was extremely encouraging and insightful.

Thanks to Connie Shaw, Editor-in-Chief of Sentient Publications. I deeply appreciate the support, friendship and confidence you offered with both *Shut-Down Learner* and *School Struggles*.

Foreword

The priority placed on education today and the competitiveness for success have made parents more aware than ever—and more anxious—about their children's progress in school. While most travel a relatively smooth road through the years of school, many children, the ones whom Dr. Selznick addresses, have a bumpier ride. As a psychologist working with children and adolescents for several decades, I have worked—and written about—those who struggle in school. These young people may be educationally challenged because of difficulties with reading, spelling, or math, or they may suffer because of ADHD or social problems. Whatever the cause, it became apparent to me years ago that their struggles in school are not confined to the 3 Rs or the classroom, but affect all aspects of their lives, and certainly their families' lives as well. When a child functions well in school, everyone reaps the rewards. But when he or she is a struggling learner, for academic, social or behavioral reasons, life becomes more difficult. Parents tend to become stressed and angry, frequently blaming their child, the school, and each other for the problems. And most of all, the child's self-esteem suffers.

Although progress has been made in identifying and treating those children who have what I refer to as "learning differences" (rather than "learning disabilities"), many issues remain to help them travel successfully through the school years. There are still too many potholes for them to traverse, and not nearly enough has been done to address the social and behavioral challenges that many youngsters face both in and outside of school. These "living disabilities" can become even more pervasive and anxiety-provoking for the child and his family than his problems with reading or math. It's hard to feel good about yourself when you are the lonely child or adolescent with no one to play with.

In *School Struggles,* Dr. Selznick covers a wide range of the common concerns related to children's learning in school, in a clear, easy-to-read style that parents and teachers will appreciate. He stresses the importance of parents' understanding their child's difficulties and gives common sense advice for them to help their child navigate the school years more successfully. I particularly enjoyed Dr. Selznick's "Try This" and his "Takeaway Points" at the end of each topic. They are concise summations for parents, clearly stated and replete with knowledge, compassion, and excellent advice. As I read this book, I wish that all children who struggle in school could have the privilege of seeing Dr. Selznick, and that all their parents would follow his suggestions. It may not be easy for those who struggle in school, but parents and teachers can help to make the road much smoother and less rocky for their children. With patience and greater understanding, they are more likely to be accepting of their children's issues and, therefore, in a better position to help. The right interventions, as portrayed in this important book, can change the learning and living landscape for children and their families.

—BETTY B. OSMAN, PH.D.,
author of *No One to Play With: The Social Side of Learning Disabilities;*
Psychologist, Department of Behavioral Health,
Child and Adolescent Service, White Plains Hospital

Introduction

——— ——— ——— ——— ——— ———

Parents worry about their children. (Well, it's mostly moms who worry about their children.) I know this because, as a child psychologist who's been working with families for over twenty-five years, I have interacted with thousands of parents who are worried about their children. The worries are over issues that span the range of childhood, from preschool through to going off to college and into young adulthood.

There are essentially two groupings of children: the Smooth Road kids and the Rough Road kids. The fortunate children going down the smoother road generally manage the academic, social, and behavioral demands of childhood throughout the different phases of their development. While these children experience some bumps in the road, they have a relatively easy ride. They receive a great deal of positive reinforcement from parents and teachers in an ongoing feedback loop of positive occurrences leading to more positive occurrences.

Then there are the children who go down a much rougher road. For them, the road is very bumpy from a young age. It is filled with potholes of academic, social, and behavioral types.

Often these are temperamentally challenging children who encounter a multitude of co-occurring problems. Among other things, these children face various academic struggles. They are the children who have trouble focusing and who are very disorganized. They are the ones who tend to be picked on by other children. They are also the ones who frequently don't get invited to birthday parties. Whatever the themes are for any individual child, for this group in general, it's a much, much bumpier ride.

It is our job as parents and professionals to try to make the road a little smoother for these kids. I have come to believe that, no matter what, the road that these children travel will always be rockier than for those on the smoother road, but I also believe that much can be done to fill in the potholes and make their ride easier.

My whole professional career has been devoted to those children traveling down the rough road. Just as in my previous book, *The Shut-Down Learner: Helping Your Academically Discouraged Child* (Sentient Publications, 2009), no quick fixes or easy solutions are offered in this book.

What is offered is perspective and, I hope, some understanding. There is a great deal that keeps parents awake with worry, and this book attempts to alleviate some of the concern. It is my belief that if the children who are going down the rockier road are better understood, the ride will be smoother. Tensions in the house will decrease. Your child's self-esteem won't be so beaten down. Small gains and improvements (in everyone, not just in the child) will lead to larger and larger gains over time.

What's This Book About?

This book covers many issues related to children's struggling in school.

Children with a school-struggling style share many characteristics that cause parents a great deal of anxiety and concern. These include:

- a sense of being increasingly disconnected, discouraged, and unmotivated relative to school
- fundamental weakness with reading, writing, and spelling that leads to diminished self-esteem and increased insecurity
- increased avoidance of school tasks, such as homework, or any academic endeavors that require sustained mental effort
- dislike and avoidance of reading
- dislike and avoidance of writing
- minimal gratification from school, even if some children (i.e., the girls) are very pleasant in their public demeanors
- social challenges

The vast majority of school-struggling children share many of these qualities, whether the child officially appears on the school's radar screen as a child classified in special education, is receiving some kind of remedial support, or is not receiving remediation at all.

School struggling is not only academic. It also includes social challenges, like how you navigate the social waters of the lunchroom or the playground. Kelsey, one of my favorite little girls whom I've known since kindergarten (she is now in fourth grade), is a wonderful, competent student. However the social dynamics of interacting with the girls in her class, as well as those of the lunchroom and playground settings, have caused her a great deal of distress, hence she is a school-struggling child. Even though she doesn't have the dislike of reading and writing that is very common, Kelsey can become quite discouraged relative to social interactions in school. Helping to keep her connected and positive has not been easy.

It is important that you don't go over the above list and say something like, "Well, my child doesn't have all these qualities, so I guess she doesn't fit the model of school struggling." These are just guidelines. From my perspective, struggling is struggling, whatever the mix of variables. This struggling creates challenges for parents that the children traveling down the smoother road do not so often present.

You may say there are a gazillion books on parenting and childhood, so what's the value of having a gazillion and one? I've never felt that anyone, even the most credentialed expert, knows in absolute terms the right answer for challenging children and challenging situations. Each child and family is different. Children come from a complex mixture of cultural and socioeconomic backgrounds that make each family unique. It would be presumptuous on the part of a professional to tell a parent how parenting should be done with their child. There are only guidelines based on years of research, professional practice, and experience.

This book attempts to discuss common concerns related to school struggling. There are excellent books on the market that focus on one individual theme, such as reading difficulty, ADHD, or organizational problems. Some of these books are mentioned in the Appendix. Are some issues and syndromes left out? Certainly. I have tried to cover a range of commonly occurring issues—especially those that frequently keep you awake at night—from a down-to earth perspective.

The material that follows is offered from my perspective. I do many public presentations, and at practically every talk I have ever given someone offers a different view or disagrees with a particular point. I welcome disagreement and enjoy talking back and forth with the parent or teacher who raises another, sometimes opposite, view. It's the same with this book. Nothing in it is meant to be taken as hard, gospel truth. It's just my view from having worked with thousands of struggling kids for many years. You can take some of it, all of it, or none of it. Human nature being what it is, it is my hope that you are largely in agreement with what I offer, but that remains to be seen.

At this point in my life I have logged many miles working with children. In some way, shape, or form I have been working with kids since I was fifteen years of age. I started as a camp counselor, then became a classroom teacher, special education teacher, reading specialist, school psychologist, psychologist, and graduate school professor. I feel that in many ways my entire career can be boiled down to one driving question:

> How can we better help the child traveling down the rough road, whether it is for academic, social, or behavioral reasons, or all of the above?

I guess I could say that's my professional mission statement.

The material that that follows is largely written as a response to that one underlying question. Typically, an individual chapter grew out of a real situation that occurred while working with a child; it was prompted by something in my professional interaction with a family.

School Struggling: The Formula

In my efforts to explain school-struggling, shut-down-learner-style kids to parents, I created a formula that shows the overall trajectory with these kids. Since I have always been mathematically challenged, I was quite proud of the high-level, algebraic (OK, it's only addition) formula that resulted. It is as follows:

Cracks in the Foundation
+ Time
+ Lack of Understanding
+ Strained Patterns of Family Communication
= School Struggling (Shut-Down Learners)

Reflecting on the formula will help you understand the thinking behind the chapters that follow, since almost all of them can be grouped within different parts of it. The formula provides a type of road map. I will briefly review each part here for further clarification.

Cracks in the Foundation. Cracks in a child's learning can be identified as early as preschool and kindergarten. Does your child have trouble learning letter names and their sounds, for example? In the first grade is the child showing difficulty in his attempts at blending sounds, which is a component building-block step that leads to later decoding skill? Is your kindergarten child unable to follow directions and instead just rolling around in circle time? Is the child aggressive or pushy in the playground? Socially withdrawn? If the answer to questions like these is yes, it doesn't mean that your young child is automatically on the road to shutting down or school struggling. However, like cracks in your house that will expand if ignored or untreated, these cracks may widen. Very often in my assessment and consultation work I see children in later grades whose cracks were present early, but they were largely ignored because of a belief that these cracks would take care of themselves ("He'll grow out of it....You know how boys are...").

Time. Many children start to receive attention much later than needed. Time is not kind to ignored cracks or identified red flags. Problems worsen. It is my general sense that time does not take care of skills that need tending, whether they are of an academic or social nature. Sure, maturity can help in some areas, and if you take the bird's-eye view the long-term trajectory for most kids is quite positive, but skill deficits need attention, not time. The basic message is that if you think something is going on with your child, it usually is, and you should act on this perception.

Lack of Understanding. From what I have seen over the years, many school-struggling children are given work on a daily basis that they simply can't handle, causing them unnecessary frustration. Effectively, they are almost always in deeper waters than their legitimate skill level can bear. This results in tremendous insecurity along with the frustration. The core lack of understanding is always revealed in statements from teachers and parents, such as:

- Ethan is such a nice boy, but if only he would pay attention more.
- Charlotte just doesn't try hard enough.
- Miles is unmotivated and seems lazy.

Parents and teachers often don't understand the core skill deficits that underlie these statements and cause the child a great deal of difficulty. For example, one fourth-grade girl, Felicia, struggled to read certain words presented in the text, such as *porcupine, passage,* and *amazement.* Since most fourth graders read silently to themselves, her teachers and parents were not aware how difficult it was to read such words and they mistakenly believed that she had a comprehension problem along with being avoidant (she hated reading). Felicia was a pleasant girl who wanted to do well in school. She didn't have a comprehension problem—the misread words just caused considerable interference in the text—and she wasn't particularly avoidant. Most humans stay away from things that they do not do well. Felicia was misunderstood. Cracks in her foundation were evident at a very young age, time was going by, and much misunderstanding was taking place.

Strained Patterns of Family Communication. School struggling pushes a family's buttons for a variety of reasons. Over time, tension mounts. Disagreements occur between parents who engage in the "You're too soft on him," "No, you're too hard on him" dance. Yelling becomes a predominant part of the household landscape. There is nothing like the daily ritual of homework struggling to raise the household temperature, with screaming and arguing becoming overused parenting tools. As you can see, the contributing variables, such as time (we have been doing this for a long time) and lack of understanding, add significantly to the strained patterns of family communication. One of the biggest issues resulting from strained communication patterns is the depletion of emotional fuel in the tank of the school-struggling, shut-down learner. For so many kids I have seen over the years, unspoken anger underlies much of their day-to-day interaction, yet this is largely unaddressed. Once the punishments have started to pile up, the anger comes out in good old-fashioned ways, such as statements like "you can't make me" or "you can't control me."

Guiding Principles

Below are the major principles or themes you will find underlying many of the chapters in this book. You will hear echoes of these principles throughout, since they guide me with children and their families:

Smooth Road and Rough Road Kids. There are the kids who have a relatively smooth ride, and then there are the rest. It's not that the smooth road children don't encounter any bumps in the road; it's just that their bumps are not so bumpy. They have an easier passage from preschool through college. Meanwhile, for the rockier road kids school can be brutal. Often they are learning at a much different pace than their peers. I am not suggesting that children on the rockier road will have *all* of the possible academic and social troubles. What I am saying is that the road is just going to be tougher, due to a host of variables and factors.

Gradations from the Middle. I am generally uncomfortable with labeling and pathologizing children. I see kids more in gradations and shades of gray. Commonly I am asked about a child, "Does he have ADHD?" "Is he dyslexic?" and other such questions. Since these syndromes occur on a continuum, it is sometimes hard to say definitively. So many children reside in the zone that is "average" by the school standards, meaning the lower portion of the average range, yet they are struggling mightily. Being in the 30th percentile in reading or in paying attention may place you on the lower portion of the average range, but it still means that a good 70 percent of the population in your comparison group is ahead of you. This is not comforting. Many of the chapters refer to these common syndromes and children who are functioning in the average range, albeit the lower portion of this range on a given variable, such as reading or paying attention.

The Soup Pot Theory of Everything. I subscribe to the soup pot theory of practically everything. What this means is that I rarely see things as one way or another, but as a mixture of variables that interact to create the challenges in children. There is a myriad of different issues for most of the children of concern. You might have a helping of ADHD, mixed in with a tablespoon of reading disability, and a dash of poor coping, resulting in a challenging brew that is hard to label. The child may not be exactly "this" or "that," but the variables place her solidly on the left side of the struggling curve—the rockier road.

Losing Our Instinct for Childhood: Need for Patience and Understanding. I sometimes think we are losing our instinct for childhood. I listen to the parents' stories about their children. I look around at things taking place and am concerned about how we view children. There is so much emphasis on pathologizing relatively normal aspects of child development. Often in our culture, patience with children is in very short supply. We want them to read when they are struggling or to act maturely when they may be immature. In so many areas kids need a lot of time and understanding. Forcing issues with children against their own natural timetable will not work, yet I see this happening often.

I believe that one of the fundamental qualities these children need from adults is *patience.*

The second overriding need of children is to be understood. I find that children are misunderstood over and over. Classic examples are the constant refrain, "If he just tried harder…" or the statement, "She's just lazy." Then there's the classic, "He has not learned to pay attention properly."

Most children want to please. If he could pay attention well, why would he choose not to?

There are lots of theories as to why things occur or don't occur with children. I believe that many of these theories stem from not understanding the child better. A lack of patience and limited understanding can contribute to many problems.

Reading, Spelling, and Writing Problems Underlie a Significant Percentage of School Struggling. The vast majority of children referred for special education are sent for assessments because of struggling in reading. If this problem could be addressed better, great sums of money would be saved through prevention. Research emphasizes early identification and treatment using sensible, structured, direct-instruction methodologies that target skill areas of concern. There has been a great deal of unnecessary controversy over the years as to what is the best approach to teaching reading. Much good research exists that highlights best practices.

Children can be identified as "at risk" for reading (and spelling and writing) at four and five years of age. Too often, though, there is a wait-and-fail mindset. Parents raising issues in kindergarten and first grade are often dismissed as being needlessly worried. The vast majority of children who struggle later and cost school districts a great deal of money could have been identified as at risk in kindergarten and first grade with powerful screening tools that would take approximately fifteen minutes to administer. While screening and identifying children early will not eliminate all of the problems schools face, many children will be placed on the right path and not face the devastating defeat that the regressive wait-and-fail approach yields.

Organizational Problems Plague Children and Strain the Family. Organizational problems, or *executive function deficits* as they are currently labeled, cause a great deal of strife in families, especially from the fourth grade and beyond. These problems lead to procrastination, forgetting to hand in work, and a general tone of academic malaise that negatively affects families. There are no magic bullets for these problems, but understanding them and providing supportive structure can reduce much of the friction that results from more reactive approaches (i.e., yelling and punishing).

Parenting Isn't the Root of All Childhood Problems. Child temperament is a crucial yet underrated variable that accounts for a great deal of the difficulty families face with challenging children. Certainly parenting counts and is a big factor, but we tend to see parenting as the be-all and end-all when it comes to child behavior. For example, I can't understand how parenting is the primary factor when there are two or three children in a family and only one of them is challenging while the other two are flexible and easy going. How the parents respond to the challenges in a given situation is certainly a large factor, and perhaps the only one that is within parental control.

Yelling Is Overdone. Yelling is overdone and overrated as a parenting tool. There are almost always built-in natural consequences that we forget to consider, leading to parental overkill in many situations. Perhaps 90 percent of the stuff that parents get emotionally drawn into is unnecessary. We are so caught up in reacting that we lose sight of the goal. Allowing natural consequences to occur while having a more pulled back, matter-of-fact posture will eliminate a considerable number of the typical struggles that take place in households and allow learning to take place.

Encouragement Does Not Come from a Computer. Teaching is relational. In this era of overemphasizing the value of test scores as the primary (if not sole) measure of teacher effectiveness, we don't talk nearly enough about the value of the teacher-child relationship. Encouragement does not come from a computer; it comes from a good relationship that the child has developed with a teacher or other adult. It is this encouragement that allows everything to take place. Without good relationships, little progress can be made. Adults who maintain a strong stance of encouragement will help kids overcome many barriers. I know of nothing that has greater impact. That is why I think of good remedial tutoring as "learning therapy." So much takes place between the teacher and the child that is immeasurable. Sadly, we are losing sight of this fact, to the great detriment of children.

Modern Children Are Far More Indulged Than We Realize. This is another intangible perception about how things are in the modern era. However, there is emerging research on the negative effects of indulging children, and I hear from educators all the time how much of a change there has been in children in the last fifteen to twenty years, most of it not for the better. The sense is that children are very self-oriented and are used to being catered to and indulged. Mounting research suggests that this is, indeed, the case. I am hearing more and more from families with children who aren't taught a very basic formula: you give and you get. What I observe with many children is: you get and don't give. There is little of that old give and take. The equation is one-sided and parents are feeling upended by their children's sense of entitlement.

Technology Is Changing the Landscape of Childhood. Go to a party or an event with teens or young adults and everyone's glued to their "screen." A mom recently described a pool party she had for her eighth-grade daughter. "It was very sad," she said. "I walked out and no one was talking to each other. They were all on their cell phones."

What is the effect of screen obsession on empathy and the ability to communicate in a relationship? How often are children able to sustain playing outside without returning to their screens? Whatever happened to playing outside from morning to evening, with virtually no adult involvement? Sadly, those days seem to be gone. My sense is that children are being deeply affected by this change.

Social issues are extraordinarily challenging for many kids. Immersing ourselves in technology does not help the fundamental skill of social development.

Social Hurdles – Extremely Challenging. Perhaps nothing is more concerning to us as parents than our child's social status. As adults, few of us ever come close to the intensity of social interactions that take place throughout the majority of a child's day. From getting on the school bus to waiting to get into the building, taking part in circle time, lining up, going to lunch, and so on, there are constant social interactions. I think we take that for granted, thinking that the child will just work her way through. For the rougher road children, normal experiences—such as being in the lunchroom or playing in the neighborhood—can be extremely challenging and disconcerting. These children need more understanding from key adults to help them better navigate the challenging social waters of school.

School-Struggling, Shut-Down Learners Revisited

One of the most gratifying results of writing *The Shut-Down Learner* has been the emails that I have received from around the country and from other countries, including Australia, Canada, Hong Kong, United Arab Emirates, and Malaysia, to name a few.

The themes of the emails are similar, even if the content of the stories is different in each one. They always reflect parental anxiety and concern over how the child is managing and the myriad hurdles he faces. Here is a sample from the emails I have received:

My son Blake struggles badly with reading. We have had him tested in school but he no longer has an IEP [individualized education program], even though he continues to struggle. He has a 504 [plan for a child with a disability] for auditory processing issues after we had him privately tested for that in third grade. The school dropped his IEP for speech and suggested we have our family doctor give him a 504 for ADHD. Our doctor disagreed. That is why we went for an audiological evaluation, and hence the 504. My friend thinks you may be able to test Blake and help us get him the help he needs. He is in fifth grade and getting some Wilson reading, but his reading teacher alerted us that the gap is getting greater. We know Blake's problem is more than "auditory processing" and we know he has a focusing problem, but we don't think it is just ADHD. There are learning problems on both sides of our families.

That email is representative of so many I have received. Blake is a classic rough-road child of the shut-down learner variety. In fact, since receiving the email, I have come to know Blake well and understand how many potholes there are in the road before him. Here's another email:

Richard, your book was spot-on regarding the educational problems that my son, Evan, faces on a daily basis during the school year. He is gifted and learning disabled, and therefore the teachers see his smarts and think he is just being lazy if he doesn't know how to complete a task that is difficult for him, such as writing, reading comprehension, or memorization. We have had Evan tested on our own by a neuropsychologist, an educational specialist, and a speech and language specialist to find out what can be done, specifically, to help Evan get through school and keep his self-esteem up (it was very low a few years ago). My husband and I understand that he is a great kid and tries his best, and that he needs to go back to the fundamentals every day in learning. But how do you get teachers, whose primary responsibility is to get all of the students to pass the government-issued standardized tests, to understand Evan and help him use his strengths to continue learning, and not just add band-aids by giving him the answers, or throwing so much work at him that my husband and I wind up having to help just so that he can get through the year and graduate?

You can sense all of the soup-pot concerns with Evan, a child I never had the opportunity to meet. The ongoing view of Evan as "lazy" while he struggles in different areas, in spite of being intellectually gifted, creates lots of challenges that will make the road a rough one for Evan. One more example:

I recently bought your book. My son was labeled with ADD, multiple learning disabilities, and behavioral problems. In your book you describe Type I and Type II readers; I'm not quite sure if my son is either. He used to be more Type I when he was younger but as he got older a friend recommended that he read books that are interesting to him (comic books, e.g., *Bone*, which he loves, or *Star Wars*). I had him read aloud and he did pretty well except for some long words he skips. I feel he has gotten better at reading, but it's still very challenging. In the meantime, do you have any pointers on how to get him to go to school? He's nine and just started in a special school. It was going OK, although they say that his test scores are all over the place. They know he's delayed but can't pinpoint how much. He is VERY easily overstimulated. I am going to venture that he is already "shut-down." This week has been particularly bad for him; he says the work is "too hard" and he doesn't understand anything. It is a daily screaming match to get him to school. I am a single parent, or I would be homeschooling him.

All of these emails convey the complexity of these issues and how challenging they can be on so many levels for the child and the parents. These emails suggest that the road can be very rough, indeed. While *The Shut-Down Learner* emphasized some children's spatial nature as a cause of their difficulties with school, *School Struggles* broadens the scope to include all children who are simply on the rougher road for any reason, with one caveat.

A Caveat

When I heard from parents regarding *The Shut-Down Learner*, many raised the issue of children with more extreme diagnoses, such as bipolar disorder or pervasive developmental disorders, including autism. I wish I could respond better to those parents, but my professional experiences with such disorders is fairly limited, and this limitation is widely reflected in my writing about the struggling children that I see. In reality, many of the kids that I see have no diagnosis. They may have a dash of this and a sprinkling of that, resulting in school struggling. From the school's point of view, though, they aren't severe enough to warrant any legitimate extra attention. There are many wonderful books and websites about children with more involved diagnoses. Some of these are mentioned in the appendix at the back of the book.

Taking the Bird's-Eye View: Finding Their Way

I have been in this business long enough to see that the vast majority of kids who have struggled in different areas for much of their school life find their way into adulthood and turn out just fine. Many of the kids I knew as young children or teenagers are now happy, productive adults. If you take the pulled back, bird's-eye view, you will see that the natural growth trajectory in most people is positive. Are there some casualties along the way? Sure, but these are rare. It should give you comfort if you are in the middle of the challenges and struggles with your child that "this too shall pass" and that things will eventually be greatly improved.

It just would be nice if these kids (and their parents) could have a slightly smoother ride.

PART ONE

Struggling on the Reading Road

Possibly nothing is more challenging to a child than to struggle in reading. Starting early in kindergarten, there are differences between the "haves" (those who start learning to read without difficulty) and the "have nots" (those who struggle early).

The differences have been well documented through the Matthew Effects, by Dr. Keith Stanovich. Essentially, the Matthew Effects refer to the rich getting richer regarding their fundamental reading skills. Some children pull farther ahead while the others fall farther behind, and the gap between them widens. Why is this so? Think of two snowballs rolling down a hill. One is the positive snowball that picks up momentum and rolls smoothly down the hill, while the other is the negative one that encounters bumps and obstacles and may get stuck in the ditch.

With the positive snowball, the children start to learn their letters in preschool, and make progress in kindergarten with letters and sounds and sight words (those words that appear with high frequency in texts). They start to enjoy reading easy Dr. Seuss books and receive a great deal of recognition from others around them (parents and teachers). As they move into first grade, they progress to reading small stories and enjoy showing off their newly acquired skills. By the end of first grade, these children have internalized the "code" and are now reading chapter books. Soon they will no longer be "learning to read," but "reading to learn." With continued reading, the sheer number of words they are exposed to increases significantly. Difficult words are easily decoded and internalized. The child's word awareness increases, along with nuances of meaning and subtleties of comprehension.

The positive snowball keeps rolling down the hill, gathering momentum, well into high school, as the child is exposed to more ideas, concepts, and factual information. There is an expansion of the child's schema—the acquired knowledge and concepts that develop largely during interaction with reading and other literacy activities. (One side note: Children with this positive snowball also tend to be adequate writers. For them there is considerable satisfaction in putting words to the page.)

Then there is the negative snowball. While preschool may be fun for these children, learning letter names and the associated sounds is difficult. The letters seem the same, and it's hard to distinguish differences between many of them, like b/d or p/g. Besides this, perceiving and knowing the sounds that go along with the names of the letters is also a chore. Already in first grade the child may start trying to cover up, because, on an intuitive level, she knows there are many kids who are getting it, while she does not. By the end of the first grade, other children are reading chapter books, and this child feels stuck in the mud. While the other children move into fully reading text, the negative-snowball child labors along. Parents and teachers, while trying to be helpful, sound increasingly tense and anxious, feelings that are frequently conveyed to the child. In third grade and upper elementary school, reading larger books is avoided and, as a result, the sheer number of words that this child is exposed to is significantly lower than that of the positive-snowball child. This child's word awareness, acquired knowledge base, and fund of information are all affected. By ninth grade, the gap between the positive-experience child and the negative one is very wide.

Reading problems is actually a misnomer, because when a child has a reading disability or dyslexia, he also has a writing and spelling problem. Reading, spelling, and writing problems are a package deal. For the negative-snowball child, as bad as reading may be, writing is even worse in terms of the child's skill level and sense of competence. This child resists writing even more than reading.

One major principle: *start as early as possible.* There is no gain in waiting. As a parent, if you think something is off, you're probably right.

The chapters to follow are commentaries on some of the struggling the child faces with reading and reading development.

Your Reading Brain

Whenever I assess children, I usually have a few standard goals, regardless of the presenting problems. The first overriding goal is to try to get a handle on the child's profile of strengths and weaknesses. The second goal is to communicate this understanding effectively to the parents. The third goal is for the child to leave the assessment feeling pretty good about the experience. So many times a child comes in having been through experiences of testing or having seen professionals that left him thinking that something was wrong with his brain. I think this is sad.

In an attempt to normalize things for the child and not have him feel odd or different, I try to use terminology that the child will understand. Instead of intimidating jargon, I use a lot of metaphors of swimming in the pool or different types of athletics. I also use the "seven intelligences" of Dr. Howard Gardner (see Dr. Gardner's work that refers to linguistic, spatial, logical-mathematical, musical, bodily-kinesthetic, interpersonal intelligences) as a framework.

The conversation might go something like this:

I know that school is very hard for you and you get really down on yourself. I know that there are times when you start to think that there is something wrong with your brain. Well, I can tell you, your brain is fine.

Most of us do a couple of things really well, some things OK, and a few things not so well. Like, your "building brain" or your "Lego brain" works really well. You can build all of these Lego cities and designs better than most people I know.

Now your "reading brain" isn't as strong, but it's something we can work on and strengthen. You have a "big word problem" and we are going to target how to read those words more easily.

I find that most kids appreciate this type of explanation and get it intuitively. They understand that their reading brain isn't so great, but I think that they find it reassuring to know that most people have highs, middles, and lows and that, in this regard, there is nothing wrong with them.

That's about it. No burdensome talk about *disability* or *disorder*. Reinforcing that a child has strengths helps put things into perspective and gives a message of encouragement with a dose of reality.

TAKEAWAY POINT

In this era, people freely use the word *disabled*. I have never been comfortable using such terminology with children. Since everyone has strengths and weaknesses, I find it more helpful to use straightforward language with children in order to normalize rather than pathologize them.

TRY THIS

When you see your child getting frustrated, try to help the child back up a little and see that there are different skills that we all have. Try to show him that everyone has skill strengths and weaknesses. Perhaps put some of these skills on a chart for him to see. Ask him to rate which ones he thinks he is good at and which he's average at or not so good at. Make sure to include non-academic skills (sports, music, social, etc.).

Dyslexia/Reading Disability and Common Sense

Caring, sensitive parents come in to see me seeking direction for their child. Reviewing the testing that's been carried out on the child, I typically identify areas of need—usually concerning the core skills of reading, spelling, and writing. Yet, more often than not the kid is not getting what he needs.

Why not?

Often because of special education regulation, the parents are told something about the child's IQ and the lack of a discrepancy between his IQ score and reading achievement levels. Additionally, there may be disregard of the skill deficit and over-emphasis on the child's attention, with the subtle suggestion (never directly offered) that the child's issues are all related to his or her need to be on medication.

I don't know about you, but if your reading skills are somewhere around the 30th percentile (meaning 70 percent of the children are better than you), for example, you probably wouldn't feel too happy or secure about it. Yet, the 30th percentile is still in the lower portion of the average range, and is therefore probably not considered to be low enough, by most school districts' standards, to be eligible for receiving special assistance (see also "School Issues: The 'Zone of No Zone'").

Regardless of whether or not you are seen as eligible for special services, if you are in the 30th percentile for word decoding and oral reading skills (reading fluency), you need help. This is common sense.

On a related note, nothing in the accepted definition of dyslexia (reading disability) mentions a discrepancy with IQ. Ask anyone you know what they think of dyslexia, and they will invariably answer, "Isn't that when you read upside down and backwards?"

Well, I have assessed thousands of kids I believe to be dyslexic and have yet to meet one who reads upside down and backwards.

To clear up any confusion, stick with this research-based definition:

Dyslexia is a specific learning disability that is neurological in origin. It is characterized by difficulties with *accurate and/or fluent word recognition*, and by poor spelling and decoding abilities. These difficulties typically result from a deficit in the phonological component of language that is often unexpected in relation to other cognitive abilities and the provision of effective classroom instruction. Secondary consequences may include problems in reading comprehension and reduced reading experience that can impede growth of vocabulary and background knowledge. (NICHD: National Institute of Child and Human Development)

Sound like anyone you know?

Notice there's no mention of upside down and backwards in the definition.

If your child is having trouble with "accurate and or fluent word recognition," those skills need targeted attention, regardless of the IQ number that has been identified.

If your child is having trouble with a sports skill, such as hitting a baseball, you get him hitting practice. Well, the same should be true with academic trouble: target the problem areas with a laser-like focus.

TAKEAWAY POINT

Common sense should prevail when it comes to reading problems; eligibility for services is not the important issue. If you answer yes to the question, "Is your child struggling with reading?" then regardless of eligibility, she needs help. With that said, it does not mean that the school will provide the help you would like your child to receive. Since the child is not viewed as deficient enough, there is no obligation for service. This means you need to seek outside help, if possible.

Old School Concept #1:
Stages of Reading Development

There are three important "old school" concepts in education and psychology that I think still apply, which I will discuss in this book. These concepts are tried and true, but are not being talked about enough in the modern era. While everyone in education circles is talking about RTI (Response To Intervention), maybe there are forgotten concepts that need revisiting.

The first old school concept is Stages of Reading Development. This concept comes to us from renowned researcher the late Dr. Jeanne Chall. She emphasized that all children (not just those who are struggling) pass through expected stages of reading development, but some children get stuck in a stage and their progress is greatly delayed. You can actually be an adult and still be in early stages of development, for example.

There are essentially five stages to understand. While the stages will be explained in greater detail, knowing exactly which stage of literacy development your child is in helps enormously as a road map for what you need to do next with your child. For example:

- A child still in Stage 0 has not yet progressed into actual word or text reading.
- If a child is in early Stage I, an emphasis on decoding is still needed.
- Stage II suggests that the child has learned a fair amount of basic decoding, but needs to practice consolidating these skills in order to develop fluency.
- If the child is in Stage III, the emphasis is on comprehension and vocabulary development.
- Stages IV and V involve the critical thinking typical of sophisticated high school and college/adult reading.

Know where your child is in his development, and apply common-sense approaches to move the child forward. That's the formula.

Armed with the information as to which stage of reading development a child is in, it's possible to make informed decisions with well-articulated goals.

The stages also answer the essential question of how "good to go" the child is at any given moment. For example, if your child is leaving Stage I and about to enter second grade, the suggestion is that the child is pretty ready for the next phase of development.

With the understanding of the stages, you will know whether the child has the requisite skills of a particular stage to be able to transition to the next stage. The next few chapters will focus on each of the stages, so that you are fully on board and understand what your child needs.

TAKEAWAY POINT

Knowing where your child is in his or her stages of reading development will provide you with a road map as to what you need to focus on with your child at any given time. Like the skill of riding a bike or learning to play the piano, one can quickly size up where a person is in their skill mastery. The same is true of reading. Does your child need decoding development? Comprehension? Vocabulary? The stages reveal the answers to those questions.

Stage 0

Stage 0 starts at birth and typically ends when the child leaves kindergarten. For a moment, disregard the current (often misguided) way that reading is presented prematurely to young children and just focus on what is expected in Stage 0.

Since the stage starts at birth, much of what is emphasized is language development. Talking to the baby, reading bedtime stories to the toddler and the preschooler, playing different games that emphasize language are all examples of wonderful Stage 0 activities.

There was a song from the 1960s called "The Name Game," which played with names and rhyming words to the names— "Shannon Shannon Fo Fannon, Banana Fannon Fo Fannon, Fee Fi Fo Fannan, Shannon."

One can do a lot worse in Stage 0 than play The Name Game over and over. Kids love it and playing the game stimulates rhyming capacity and the skill called phonemic awareness.

Phonemic awareness has been shown in research to be the single greatest contributor to early reading development. The skill represents the ability to play with sounds (e.g., "Say *take*." "Now say *take*, but don't say the *T*.") About half the population of five-year-olds understand this intuitively and say "ake," and about half don't get the idea at all.

Another contributor to early struggling with reading is difficulty with letter naming and the sound that goes with each letter.

For a child to be good to go out of Stage 0, they need to know their letter names cold (not just the alphabet song) and to know the sound of each letter. To leave Stage 0, it is probably good for the child to also know a handful of high frequency (sight) words such as *cat, stop, come, book*.

Do not be too fast to move out of Stage 0. Spend time stimulating and exposing the child to many of these early concepts, and this will pay dividends in the later stages of actual reading instruction and development.

TAKEAWAY POINT

Stage 0 is a fun stage filled with play and song. Do not get hung up on accelerating the reading instruction. Let the games and songs predominate. These activities will stimulate the language system that underlies reading development.

TRY THIS

If your child is three, four, or five years of age, get a hold of lyrics to "The Name Game." Sing it a lot. Your child will love it and you will be well on your way to stimulating rhyming skill and phonemic awareness. Another great thing to do in this stage is to read books aloud to your child, especially ones that are lyrical, rhythmic, and include rhyming. Much of Dr. Seuss and books such as *Chicka Chicka Boom Boom*, are good examples. There are many books of this type on the market. Don't be afraid of repetition or boredom (for the child). You can play "The Name Game" or read those books hundreds of times and your child will not get bored, and the gains in language development will be considerable.

- -

Kindergarten Mom: "Help! My child is shutting down!"

Anxiety over your child's school-based problems can start very early. A mom recently contacted me after reading *The Shut-Down Learner*.

"My son is drowning in school. Do you think he could be a shut-down learner?"

After asking a few more questions, I was struck by the fact that the child in question was only in kindergarten.

When I wrote *The Shut-Down Learner*, I was envisioning a disconnected, shut-down teenager. However, as I gave more talks to parents, many of the concerns being raised were about young children. This led me to understand that so much of the import of *The Shut-Down Learner* is to determine how we can prevent this shutting down from happening as early as possible.

Cracks in the foundation can appear very early and can be easily identified by four or five years of age. Classic Stage 0 (see "Stage 0" chapter) cracks include weaknesses with identifying letters and their sounds, along with difficulty with language-based tasks, such as rhyming.

When the cracks are ignored, time goes by and typically there is a sense that the issues are widening and getting more significant and difficult to manage.

Targeting letter naming and sound identification with good individualized instruction would be very appropriate if your child has been shown to have some of these cracks in kindergarten.

There is no gain in waiting.

TAKEAWAY POINT

Start early. While your child might not technically be shut down when he is in kindergarten or first grade, acting early is a key factor in heading off later shut-down qualities and further school struggling.

TRY THIS

If you are the parent of a Stage 0 child and you do not feel that she is progressing properly, try to find a learning specialist in your community who is oriented to these issues. The person does not have to do a very extensive testing battery, but a screening of the key areas (i.e., letter naming, phonemic awareness) is strongly recommended.

Stage I: Getting on the Bike

Stage I of reading development typically corresponds to the end of kindergarten through the end of first grade. This is the first major learning-to-read stage. Your child usually leaves the preschool stage (Stage 0) by the end of kindergarten and starts Stage I when she can do the following:

- Automatically recognize all upper- and lower-case letters in isolation when randomly presented.
- Know the appropriate sounds associated with the letters.
- Know a handful of high-frequency words (i.e., sight words—those that appear frequently in a text).

I sometimes explain Stage I to parents as being akin to learning how to ride a bike. In the beginning of Stage I the child will be shaky for quite some time. He may start to fall off, but you are there to provide support. Stage I reading development is very much like this progress in bike riding skill. There will be much insecurity at the start, with more and more confidence following. Stage I is a crucial stage of development; it is the foundation upon which all later reading skills are supported. *This is not a stage to rush through quickly.* It is crucial that the child has mastered the fundamental skills of this stage.

To help children progress in Stage I, the following tips should prove useful:

- Practice a lot of sight words. There are lists available that help organize these high-frequency words (see Appendix). Try playing different word games like Go Fish or a word matching game.
- Expose the child to words that follow consistent patterns, starting with one-syllable, closed-vowel words that have a consonant-vowel-consonant pattern (e.g., set, got, fit, hat). Then you can move on to more complex, one-syllable words (e.g. flat, grip, stomp, hunch).

- Stay away from multisyllabic words (e.g., largest, porcupine, calendar) during Stage I, unless the word is taught as a high-frequency sight word (e.g., little or summer).
- Give the child reading material that controls for the type of words in the text. At this stage, the reading material should have a small number of high-frequency (sight) words mixed in with one-syllable words with closed vowels, as noted above. Lots of early Dr. Seuss books are very good for this (for example, *Cat in the Hat*).
- Let your child read aloud to you material that is easy for her, for about ten minutes per night.
- Keep it light and fun. Watch for any tension leaking into the reading-aloud session. Your job is to help boost confidence at this point.

If the teacher hands out worksheets or reading material that is above your child's level, politely talk to the teacher and tell her that working at frustration level is not appropriate.

TAKEAWAY POINT

Stage I is like learning to ride a bike—this is a wobbly stage. There will be little fluency in this stage. Be patient and expose your child to simple word patterns. Don't mix in too many large, multisyllabic words; those words are for later stages.

TRY THIS

Get a hold of easy Dr. Seuss books. Read them frequently with your child. Put some of the words that are in the book on index cards in bold, red magic marker. Practice the words in playful ways. Emphasize the words that follow consistent rules (i.e., short vowel words that are one syllable, such as cat, back, fish, Ted). Put the words out on the table and have the child find them by pointing or handing them to you—"Find me *fish*." Make sure the child says the word as he hands it over or points to it. Keep it fun, playful, and light.

Stage II: Riding the Bike

Stage II of reading development is an exciting time, especially if the child is in this stage at the expected time—usually beginning in second grade and ending in the middle of third grade.

In this stage, your child has mastered most of the high-frequency (sight) words and can read these automatically. He is also is starting to show a pretty good understanding of one-syllable word patterns and their component sounds. Words like *fling, stomp, branch,* and even a nonsense word like *grimp* are good examples of words that early Stage II children should be able to easily decode.

Continuing with the metaphor of the bike, you can think of Stage II as the one where the child starts out a bit insecure, but with more and more practice gains much greater confidence and fluidity to the point where the child is independently enjoying the activity.

The primary activity of Stage II is reading—lots of it—both out loud and silently, with small chapter books that are fairly easy (but not too easy) for the child to read independently. While in the early stages too many large words would overwhelm the child, as the child progresses through the stage she will be able to manage more of these words efficiently and read them correctly.

In this stage it is useful to help a child to break low-frequency words down into component parts and to practice this skill using index cards (see "Simple Low-Frequency Word Strategy"). Low-frequency words are ones that do not show up all that often in the text. Even if the child knows the meaning of the word immediately, the word is not a sight word or a high-frequency word. Low-frequency words include the following: *sweater, cave, dinosaur, parrot.* Most Stage II children would know the meaning of these words, but reading them successfully may be a different story.

Along with regular out-loud reading practice, reviewing this growing list of low-frequency words will start moving your child out of Stage II.

You will know that your child is starting to leave Stage II when he knows almost all of the high-frequency words automatically and can read text containing less controlled word patterns fairly smoothly. The child demonstrates much greater confidence with more difficult word patterns, and "decoding" becomes a backdrop issue. The child is "riding the bike" independently.

TAKEAWAY POINT

The key to Stage II is practice and more practice. Think of a piece of music that you can play, but you still need to play it a lot for it to become effortless. Ultimately, the goal of sophisticated reading skill is for word recognition and fluency to be second nature. Practice is the only way for it to become effortless. Have your child read aloud to you often (fifteen minutes a night, for example), but make sure that the text is not too challenging.

TRY THIS

Pick a story of the week. Think of the story like a song that needs practicing. This will be the story that is read aloud each night. Give your child a marble to put in a jar or make a check on a calendar each time he reads the story. Set up a point system for later cashing these in for prizes.

"Mom! There's Lincoln Whatever Field"

Should a bright fifth grader be able to read the word *financial?* Well, when driving by the Philadelphia Eagle's stadium, fifth-grader Carrie got excited when she saw the stadium with the sign that read: Lincoln Financial Field.

The problem was, Carrie couldn't read the word *financial.* Instead she said, "There's Lincoln *Whatever* Field!"

Carrie's parents have been bringing their concerns to school personnel since Carrie was in third grade. Seeing her nightly struggles with difficult words, they wondered whether she may have dyslexia.

In response to their concerns, they've been told repeatedly:

- She's so sweet. She's such a hard worker.
- We don't believe in dyslexia.
- She comprehends so well. She can't have a problem.

Many bright kids can comprehend, even if they do not read words well. It's like playing tennis—you can win many games with a good forehand while covering up your weak backhand. Carrie does that while reading. She is smart enough to cover up her weaknesses, and the fact that she's so sweet really doesn't help her.

To draw another parallel, recently I was listening to a webinar lecture. The problem was that the audio frequently cut out, making it difficult, but not impossible, to follow. While I missed a lot of information, I caught enough to get by.

That's what reading is like for Carrie. Probably every tenth word or so cuts out and becomes *whatever* while she plugs along and tries not to get noticed. She can bluff by answering enough questions to show that she comprehends.

I don't know how you see it, but it seems like a problem to me when a fifth grader has to substitute *whatever* when reading a word like *financial.* It strikes me as a problem that needs attention.

It really is beyond my "comprehension" how anyone can view that as adequate reading.

TAKEAWAY POINT

Do not let educators or other professionals tell you things like, "The only thing that matters is comprehension" or "We really don't know what dyslexia is." If you are in society and can't decode everyday words like *financial* in the above example, you are handicapped. The same is true for any text material beyond the fifth-grade level, as these levels contain many large, unfamiliar words.

Stage III: Independently Riding the Bike

Once your child is in Stage III of reading development, he has reached the Promised Land or, to put it another way, is now bicycling independently and enjoying the ride. Sadly, many adults (including those with dyslexia who remained unremediated) never reach this stage. In fact, the prisons are filled with people who could never reach Stage III, and thus found school incredibly frustrating.

Why is Stage III the Promised Land? Because at this stage no longer are you "learning to read." The vast majority of print, whether in magazines, books, or online, is available to you in terms of its basic readability. You join the ranks of people who have fundamental literacy skills.

When statistics on countrywide literacy rates are bandied about and significant numbers of people are classified as illiterate, what this really means is that these people have never been able to get out of Stage I or II of reading development.

As a parent of a Stage III child, you should concentrate on developing your child's broad array of comprehension skills (e.g., higher-order reasoning and drawing conclusions), along with enhancing his or her reading and speaking vocabulary. Writing development is also a good focus for Stage III.

What's exciting about Stage III readers is that they're no longer hampered by the more mechanical aspects of the text found in Stage I and part of Stage II, and their mental energy is not bottlenecked with issues of decoding or reading fluency. As Dr. Jean Chall noted, from Stage III forward a person is no longer "learning to read, but reading to learn."

TAKEAWAY POINT

As a parent of a child in Stage III, now that phonics, decoding, and reading fluency are a thing of the past, you can encourage broad reading with an array of different subject matters. Try to establish a nightly hour of family reading time. Talk about the ideas in the books, read books together, and get excited.

Stages IV and V: Sophisticated Readers

Once a child has spent a number of years (e.g., grades four through early high school) in Stage III, he has theoretically been exposed to a great deal of reading material. There has been an increase in vocabulary and, through a range of writing activities, higher-order thinking skills have been developed.

In a solid Stage IV (high school), students must deal with more than one viewpoint. Topics in textbooks are approached from multiple perspectives and treated in greater depth. Dealing with more than one set of facts, competing theories, and varied interpretations provides knowledge of how to acquire new points of view and increasingly complex concepts. Study skills and practice in efficient reading are beneficial at this stage.

Stage V (age eighteen and above) is the highest stage of reading development. This should be thought of as sophisticated college-level reading, through the rest of one's life. Stage V readers can understand materials in the degree of detail and completeness that is needed to serve their purposes. Readers select materials deliberately; they know what not to read as well as what to read. They analyze, synthesize, and make judgments about what they read. They balance their own comprehension of the words with their analysis of the content and their own ideas about the topic. At this stage, reading is constructive. The reader constructs knowledge and understanding from reading what others have written.

Old School Concept #2: Instructional Level

Remember we talked earlier about Old School Concept #1 (Stages of Reading Development). The second old school concept that isn't talked about enough is instructional levels.

A child's instructional level is an important concept to understand, and it's not just about school. It applies to many day-today activities (e.g., knowing how to make a bed), as well as academic tasks, but is of particular importance in a child's reading development.

There are three instructional levels:

- **Independent level** means the task is easy for the child, and no assistance is needed to perform the task
- **Instructional level** means she can mostly do the task, but needs a degree of assistance
- **Frustration level** means the task is simply too hard for the child, even with assistance.

Using a non-academic example, let's say seven-year-old Martha comes to you and says, "Mommy, I want to make my own lunch." On the one hand, you are thrilled that she is taking the initiative, but on the other you know she isn't yet able to do this task independently. You don't want to squash her spirit, but letting her work in her frustration level will have the same effect. You know she will need some support and guidance.

For any tasks the child faces, whether reading a chapter book, managing a worksheet, sitting still in church, making lunch, making a bed, or crossing the street, ask yourself the following questions:

- Can the child do the task without any assistance? If the answer is yes, that's the *independent level.* When it comes to reading, listen to the child; if she reads smoothly and understands what she reads, she is in the independent level.
- Is some assistance needed? That's the *instructional level.* With regard to reading, she may need help pronouncing some words or understanding certain words or concepts.

- Is the task over the child's head? That's the *frustration level.* Children at frustration level read in a labored and strained manner, and seem to not to get many of the concepts.

Too many of the kids I see are swimming in frustration level waters. Read the signs:

STAY OUT!

ROUGH WATERS!

DROWNING LIKELY!!!!

TAKEAWAY POINT

It is essential to understand a child's instructional level. Simply stating that a child is in level "G" (from one reading series) or in the "Proficient" range (as noted on standardized testing) does not provide enough information. Pinpoint which level is easy for your child, and which level is appropriate for him to receive instruction. Know what level is too difficult to manage. Knowing your child's instructional level is especially important when it comes to reading development, and this will help to guide your interventions.

TRY THIS

Every once in a while with the material your child gets from school, pick a random part of the story or chapter and ask the child to read out loud. You only need a page or two to get a sense of the child's capacity to manage the text. If the child is reading in a strained and labored manner or if she is making many errors (such as word substitutions), it is important to let the teacher know that the work is over the child's head.

Brief Tip: Get Clear on Your Focus with Reading Remediation

There are essentially two types of reading problems:

- **Type I:** The child has trouble decoding words and reading fluently.
- **Type II:** The child can read fluently, but has difficulty understanding what is read.

If you are seeking remediation through tutoring, get clear on what you are targeting; don't scattershot your remediation.

Is the tutoring tailored to emphasize decoding/fluency or comprehension? It is not sufficient for the teacher to say that "I do a little of this and a little of that." The time is too precious and the typical tutoring hour too expensive to not know what the emphasis will be.

If the tutor is not clear, she needs to get clear; otherwise you may want to find a different tutor.

Good testing data should help you get clear on what you need to have emphasized.

Be laser-focused in your approach so you can hit the right target.

Listen to the Moms

Over the last thirty years, research in education and psychology that is focused on reading disabilities produces one consistent truth—early identification and intervention trumps waiting and acting later. The title of Dr. Joseph Torgesen's seminal article on this topic, "Catch Them Before They Fall," says it all.

Who are the best people to identify problems early? Pediatricians? Psychologists? Neurologists? Teachers?

Nope. The moms.

In my view, 99 percent of the time when the mom thinks that something is wrong with her child, there is something wrong. It is the rare mom who is mistaken about this.

Yet often when the moms raise the issue of their late-preschool, kindergarten, or first-grade child, they tend to get messages like these:

- You're worrying too much.
- There are many late bloomers.
- You know how boys are.
- We really can't tell what's going on until third grade.

Not being professionals in the field, the moms accept these messages and stifle their worries.

But rather than suffering through the agony of waiting until third or fourth grade, so many kids could be identified by early screening and given services, as suggested by Dr. Torgesen. Screenings do not take a lot of time, money, or effort; some fifteen minutes per child can identify those at risk for learning/reading problems at the ages of four, five, and six years. Sadly, these screenings are not occurring in many schools, despite all of the research and clinical knowledge that exists.

A mom recently said to me, "Look. Where there's smoke, there's fire. I know my kid is struggling. He's in third grade and I keep getting put off. For what purpose?"

There is no purpose. Why let the fire smolder and build to the point where it is overwhelming? At the first signs of smoke, it's time to act. It's not time to panic but to take an effective action, like identifying the child's stage of reading development and deciding which area you are going to target (see "Brief Tip: Get Clear on Your Focus with Reading Remediation").

You don't need to be a psychologist or a reading specialist to know when a child is struggling. On a nightly basis, moms see the effort that goes into getting through a reading assignment or a difficult worksheet. This is something moms get intuitively.

One solution: listen to the moms and take early action. Waiting and seeing what will happen is not an option.

TAKEAWAY POINT

Moms, trust your gut, especially with early reading development. If you are concerned, take action if possible. Seek outside help in the form of testing and remedial tutoring if you do not feel that the school is stepping up to the plate. Don't listen to messages such as, "He will grow out of it." Rarely does that happen.

All Aboard the Curriculum Ship

Is your child falling off the Curriculum Ship?

Leaving the dock in early September, the Curriculum Ship keeps steering its course until mid- to late June, when it arrives at a port somewhere on the other side of the ocean. This is not a ship that slows down, even if some of its passengers are falling overboard.

No, the ship must go full steam ahead.

Cara, age nine, is barely treading water while she watches the ship leave her behind. Upset by what is happening in school, Cara's mom said, "This week they are reading science stories about photosynthesis. Photosynthesis!! She can't read or pronounce the word! She has no idea what's going on. The teacher handed back Cara's worksheet packet all marked up as wrong. Cara was beside herself—she felt horrible. How can a nine-year-old deal with all of this failure?"

Looking at the sheets, I could feel my blood pressure rising again. Besides *photosynthesis,* there were many other words on the page that Cara could not read on her own. Clearly, she was in over her head.

"She can't handle the stories," I told the mom. "Many of these words are far beyond her ability."

"I know," she responded. "It took her two hours to complete the worksheets last night, and she still got an F, along with one of those unhappy faces at the top of the sheet. Can you imagine?"

"It's the Curriculum Ship," I tell her. "The message is 'swim harder if you want to keep up with the ship.' No support."

Rough waters, indeed.

Do whatever you can to keep your child afloat, even if she is being tugged along in a life preserver. The Curriculum Ship doesn't bother to consider which passengers have fallen overboard and need to be rescued. The ship must reach the other side. That is its mission.

TAKEAWAY POINT

Chances are, if your child is one of those traveling the rough road, he has a variety of academic needs that are difficult to resolve. Too often these children are mired in frustration-level work that they cannot handle without tremendous adult support. No one (adult and child alike) can function at frustration level. If the work is too hard and the Curriculum Ship is forging ahead, you need to speak up and politely let the child's teacher know that the work is frustrating and too difficult. If the teacher does not show understanding, then you need to speak to the school's administration.

Messages from the Life Boats

When I first wrote about the Curriculum Ship, it generated a fair amount of reaction from teachers and parents. Here is a sampling of the responses. The first is from an elementary school teacher:

Hence the creation of differentiated instruction, which, on paper, sounds great but when you're dealing with 26+ in a classroom, the likelihood of a teacher, even a veteran teacher, doing this successfully is not good. We need to look at the curriculum and possibly go back to the A and B classes so that children are not hampered by slower learners and slower learners can feel as if they can succeed at their own pace.

Differentiated instruction has been in vogue for some time. It is the theory that various ability levels and learning styles can all interact in the same classroom, with the teacher customizing instruction to meet the variety of needs and skill levels.

Another comment came from Amy, a fourth-grade teacher:

I just wanted to let you know that the Curriculum Ship was a great analogy for my students. It is so true—we are merely keeping them afloat, hoping that they will hang in there.... It is sad, but true, that some of my students will let go of the life preserver soon. While they may make it in fifth grade, they probably won't much more after that!

Pat, a mother of a twelve-year-old who has struggled over the years, said:

It's too bad that parents aren't tutored in knowing what size life preservers to keep on hand for their children! As the curriculum gets more difficult, it seems the theory of one size fits all for the curriculum could not be more in error! If this ship is sailing along steadily, ignoring who has gone overboard, you would think someone would notice and sound an alarm! Instead, we blame the child for not trying hard enough—and treading water in deep seas will only keep you alive for so long!

I believe that all of these points are valid. The differentiated instruction theory, while still very popular, would seem to be extraordinarily difficult for a teacher. Staying with the water metaphor, how does one work with a group in the deep end of the pool while others are floundering in the shallow end?

I guess, as Amy says, you are just trying to keep them afloat, but that isn't satisfying, is it? The sanctity of the curriculum and its one-size-fits-all nature is also frustrating to the strugglers. They just can't keep up.

TAKEAWAY POINT

The issue of the never-slowing Curriculum Ship is one that teachers often recognize, but feel helpless to address because of differentiated instruction. It is very challenging for teachers and often results in children falling off the ship and being left behind. Mind you, the alternative of more groupings that were more homogenous in skill level also created its own set of problems. This issue of classroom makeup (similar abilities vs. mixed abilities) has never been fully resolved.

Was This a Problem that Could Have Been Averted?

The mom of Alison, a fifth-grade child who had some reading issues (decoding, fluency, etc.) asked, "Was this a problem that could have been averted?"

My answer:

There are powerful screening measures that can be given early on (in kindergarten or first grade) that take about fifteen minutes per child to complete. From the screening, three essential groups would be identified:

- **Green Zone Kids:** those who are good to go (about 60 percent of the population)
- **Yellow Zone Kids:** those who show some concerning signs (about 30 percent)
- **Red Zone Kids:** those who show significant to severe signs of difficulty (about 10 percent)

For the 40 percent showing concerning signs, merely giving them the regular curriculum (stories, literature, whole language, etc.) is not adequate. The kids in the Yellow and Red Zone need much more structured, sequential approaches to reading development. Just because a child is in the Yellow Zone doesn't necessarily mean the child is "learning disabled." It does mean that she needs assistance and without this assistance the problems will widen.

Unfortunately, for the Alisons of the world, these kids are often not screened, nor are they given structured approaches. They read literature and stories that have no discernible, layered sequence of skill mastery. Then in the later grades they stand on a foundation of soft balsa wood.

It seems to be a fairly easy model to implement. So many children would avoid falling through the cracks and receive what they need at a very early age.

TAKEAWAY POINT

Even if the school does not do the type of screening that is being suggested here, you may want to consult with someone in your community who does this type of work. A psychologist oriented to education may be a good start. There are a number of instruments on the market that are typically given by psychologists that can help to screen children in the manner being suggested. A reading specialist may also be someone to consider if a psychologist is not easily accessed.

Vision and Learning

James, twelve, hates reading and has avoided it as much as he can over the years. There are the nightly battles where James' parents try to insist that James read for twenty to thirty minutes, while

James reacts in anguish that he won't do it. Or if he does, he fakes the reading by mouthing words to himself. James complains that reading makes him tired.

Evelyn, age fourteen, likes reading but whenever she starts reading material of any reasonable length, she tends to give up, saying her eyes hurt when she reads. Her parents have questioned her motivation. They keep pushing her to "try harder."

When I evaluated both of these kids, there was a common theme. Neither of these children had the Stage I or Stage II issues of decoding or word reading difficulty. Yet, when I asked them to read lengthy passages out loud, their reading sounded strained and labored, like a weak car engine chugging up a steep hill. Also, they did not do well on any of the non-reading tasks that involved rapid left-to-right tracking and processing of information.

As a result, I referred them for a follow-up visual evaluation. This evaluation revealed that the children had adequate 20/20 vision, yet all measures of visual tracking were well below average.

The reading process is complex and many factors can affect performance. For kids like James and Evelyn, even though their reading skills have developed, their visual tracking needs to be addressed. Working on their tracking and improving their visual efficiency with eye teaming exercises (conducted by a developmental optometrist) enables them to focus more efficiently on a line of print. Such exercises do not teach a child to read but help to reduce a level of interference.

TAKEAWAY POINT

Many factors contribute to difficulty with reading and motivation. Ask your child if his eyes get tired or sore during reading or homework, or if the words on the page get blurry or move around. Consider seeing a vision specialist if you hear these kinds of complaints. Understand that any visual treatments offered are not going to teach a child to read. They can, however, put a child in a better position so he does not get as fatigued with near point processing and tracking of information.

Low-Frequency versus High-Frequency Words

Is your child struggling with reading? If the answer is yes, there are some basic concepts that are important to embrace. Understanding the concept of high-frequency versus low-frequency words is important.

The vast majority of children who struggle with reading have difficulty with low-frequency words—words that appear only seldom in the text. (Those children struggling with low-frequency words are probably in later Stage I or early Stage II of reading development.)

In contrast, high-frequency words (sometimes called sight words) appear quite often in most reading selections. Approximately 60 percent of the English language is made up of these words, so they are certainly important for your child to master.

Even if the child has mastered high-frequency words, the rubber really hits the road with the low-frequency words. Often a word's meaning is familiar to the child, but reading the word automatically and efficiently is difficult.

Let's take a word like *porcupine*. When shown a group of four animal pictures and asked to identify which one is the porcupine, the vast majority of elementary age children will get the answer right. So knowledge of the concept of *porcupine* is not the issue.

However, a child can literally go from grades one through five and never see the word *porcupine*, or if the word does appear it will be extremely seldom.

The weak decoders—those struggling with low-frequency words—look at a word like this and have no strategy or approach to deal with it. Typically, such children try to access the word from memory, like they would a high-frequency word. But since they've seen the word so infrequently, it has not been filed away as a known word for automatic retrieval.

This is why it's so crucial to have direct instruction in decoding principles—learning to break down tough words into parts. Once a child is in Stage II (see "Stage II: Riding the Bike"), it is imperative that they be taught how to break down multisyllabic words into their component parts and to blend them more efficiently. When the child does not have this skill internalized, reading remains a laborious chore, something he will want to avoid at all costs.

TAKEAWAY POINT

Low-frequency words are the tough ones for struggling readers. In many ways, learning to break these tough words down into parts is the main hurdle for them to overcome. Do not start working on these words until the child is solidly out of Stage I. However, once she is in Stage II, direct instruction and practice with longer low-frequency words is critical. Don't worry as much about comprehension until this skill is mastered (see "Stage III: Independently Riding the Bike"). Give this skill a laser-like focus and practice.

TRY THIS

Open up a representative book that is in a fifth- to sixth-grade range. Perhaps try opening a social studies book, as they usually include many low-frequency words. Scan a couple of pages and sample some of the more complex, multisyllabic words. Put these words on a list or on index cards. Have the child read them. How smooth is the reading? Was it fairly effortless? If so, then the likelihood is that the low-frequency words are not an issue at this point. If there is effort in the reading of the words, then work with multisyllabic word reading still remains to be done.

Simple Low-Frequency Word Strategy

Now that we understand how difficult low-frequency words can be for your child, let's review a simple approach to practicing these types of words. I'll go through this approach in a step-by-step manner. For materials, you'll need a box of index cards, and it's also helpful to have alphabetic divider tabs in the box.

- As you're going over your child's reading or worksheets, any word that she stumbles on will be entered on an index card. Let's say the word *dinosaur* is hard for the child to decode. Have her write out the word with a red sharpie pen on the index card.
- Underline in yellow highlighter the parts: di no saur.
- While holding up the card so it's visible to the child, ask her what sound is made by "d-i?" *di.* "That's right! And 'n-o' makes what sound?" *no.* "Great. And s-a-u-r?" *saur.* "You got it. And what's the word?" *dinosaur!*

Play with word parts like this, but make sure that you always ask for the full word at the end. As the child's word bank increases, she will start to internalize the skill of breaking the words down. She will also be filing away the words into her memory banks (see "Stage II: Riding the Bike"). While you are not turning this into a pure flash-card drill, the reinforcement and practice will help.

You should do this activity with your child for about ten to fifteen minutes a night. Over time, the child's index-card box will have grown considerably. Many word parts and larger words will have been practiced.

One last note: There's no need to turn this activity into a detested drag for the child. Instead, try keeping a chart on which you can put a stamp or star for good effort, and then after ten or so words have been completed, celebrate so the child will stay motivated and this exercise won't feel like an onerous chore. Keep the rewards lively and varied, but don't resort to offering large monetary rewards. Taking the child out for an ice-cream treat of her choice is a good example of the type of reinforcement that is appropriate to this level.

(For a more formal program utilizing an approach like this, see the "Glass Analysis for Decoding" by the late Dr. Gerald Glass (see www.glassanalysis.com), the original developer of this method. While it is not used very much in educational circles at this point, the method could be helpful to you as a parent and it is easy to follow.)

TAKEAWAY POINT

Low-frequency words are extremely challenging for struggling readers. Breaking the words down is a skill that takes a lot of practice over time. A simple, low-cost approach using index cards, with a few minutes of practice a night, can be highly productive in helping the child to internalize this skill. If you are feeling insecure in this approach as a parent, find a teacher or tutor who understands this methodology. Some tutors are not grounded in this type of work and are much more literature-based. For this type of work, you need someone with a "decoding mindset."

— —

"Daddy's tied up in traffic"

Many struggling kids have great trouble with facets of language that others take for granted.

Take Emma, age eight. One night Emma was told by her mother that her father was "tied up in traffic." Emma burst into tears. "Why is daddy being tied up?" she sobbed.

It took her mother some time to explain to Emma that her father wasn't literally being tied up, and that this was an expression commonly used when people are stuck in traffic.

So many kids have difficulty with the subtle and not-so-subtle aspects of language. Kids like Emma can be easily overloaded with too many words hitting them at once and no place in their mental closet to store such words and expressions. The effect of having difficulty with metaphorical language usually appears with reading comprehension. Such difficulty appears with inferencing, reading between the lines, and drawing conclusions.

We use language very freely, and quite often it just washes over the kid's head. Is it any wonder that so many shut-down learner kids appear distracted and zoned out in class?

So, if your child is not "steering her boat" or is "wandering in the desert aimlessly" or "spinning her wheels in the mud," perhaps you need to back up and check out your language! Perhaps you are using too many metaphors or language that is just too hard to manage.

TAKEAWAY POINT

Is your child someone who has trouble with too much language? Does she seem confused when you use figurative language? As adults, there are many phrases that we take for granted, but that go over a child's head and result in confusion. If this is the case, you may need to back up and make sure your child is "on board." Take nothing for granted with the language that you use.

TRY THIS

If your child is decoding well and reading fluently, meaning she is now in Stage III of reading development, you may need to be targeting comprehension skills, such as metaphoric language. Understanding figurative language can be difficult for children. You may want to target the child's skill in this area by having a figurative language example of the week. While driving along, for example, you may want to say something like, "You know we can kill two birds with one stone by going to this store." Without overdoing it, try to elicit from your child what the expression might mean. Use the phrase a couple of times during the course of the week.

Hmmm, Let Me Think About It...

One of the toughest tasks facing children who are solidly in Stage III of reading development is to improve their higher-order thinking skills. In this stage, a couple of terms often used in psychology may be helpful with regard to aspects of reading comprehension: *crystallized intelligence* and *fluid reasoning*.

Crystallized intelligence refers to information one has already acquired, essentially factual knowledge. For example, a crystallized fact that a child may know is that there are fifty states. This fact is either known or not known; it is not something that is reasoned.

With fluid reasoning there is reasoning (as the name implies), as well as evaluative thinking and problem solving. Contrary to a crystallized intelligence question, a fluid reasoning question is not a know-it-or-don't-know-it proposition.

Many kids I see are weak in this skill of fluid reasoning, whether it manifests with reading or with other problems. For example, let's say I ask a child to put together a bunch of blocks to match a complex pattern (a task that is on the cognitive portion of the psychological assessment). To arrive at a solution, the child would have to apply reasoning. There would need to be a connection between the internal voice in the mind of the child and the actions that lead to a solution.

I call this the "Hmm, let me think about it" voice that drives problem solving. This type of thought process also shows up with the "why?" questions that are so common in reading comprehension (e.g., "Why did the settlers decide to leave the village?") If the child is not very effective in the use of the internal voice that says, "Hmm, let me think about it," then he may reach a quick conclusion that he can't do a problem or carry out a task. Effectively, what happens is the person quickly gives up or answers, "I don't know."

Children to whom this type of thinking does not come naturally need to be encouraged, with a great deal of coaching and practice, to use the "Hmmm, let me think about it" voice. Do not assume that this voice will be there naturally as a part of the child's repertoire. Many of the children I see are very weak in this skill of reasoning and problem solving.

To help develop this internal voice and skill, you may want to watch for signs of this voice being used in real-life situations. Let's say your child faces a problem between him and a friend that is not readily solved. Pushing the use of the "Hmm, let me think about it" voice encourages fluid reasoning. You might say something like, "Well, there isn't an immediate solution to your problem with your friend, but what might you try to do to solve it?" This process shows the child that there isn't an easy answer, but by considering and reasoning, he might arrive at a solution.

Or, while the child is reading, look for ways of asking questions that don't have an easy answer, and that encourage the child to read between the lines and utilize fluid reasoning.

You might engage the child about a story, asking, "Why do you think the boy ran away from school?"

A child not wired for this type of thinking may quickly respond, "I don't know— it doesn't say."

You could continue, "Well, what are the clues? What is the evidence that might give you an answer?"

This type of back-and-forth dialoguing may help develop this thinking and can sensitize kids to increasing their "Hmm, let me think about it" internal voice. Over time you may become amazed at how reflective your child has become. You may even be on the road to having a facile problem-solver on your hands!

TAKEAWAY POINT

Many children are not naturally oriented to problem solving, an important skill in reading comprehension and in life. There are many opportunities for encouraging this skill so that it can become more natural for your child to employ. Starting in third and fourth grade (or even younger depending upon the child), watch for opportunities to help your child utilize his "Hmm, let me think about it" thought process.

TRY THIS

Look for opportunities to ask your child questions such as "Why do you think..." The question suggests that there is no right or wrong answer. If your child just shrugs, as is certainly common with middle-school children (especially the boys), try to push it a little. Remind the child that there is no right or wrong answer but you are interested in his or her opinion and what he thinks. Who knows, the child may even ask you what *you* think.

Questioning to Encourage Comprehension

Comprehension at its finest is an interactive process. The interaction takes place between the ideas, concepts, images, etc., in the text and one's own background experience, fund of knowledge, level of word awareness, and motivation, among other things. Comprehension is also compromised by poor reading fluency.

Those who comprehend best are bringing their own experiences to what they read, allowing for deeper levels of understanding.

Comprehension can be improved through many different ways. Among the most important is to increase a child's word awareness or fund of vocabulary. Vocabulary is a cornerstone skill of reading comprehension. The appendix suggests a number of different books that can be helpful with developing vocabulary.

Additionally, helping a child to infer or "read between the lines" is also beneficial. Look for ways to go beyond the facts in a text as the child reads. Without becoming too bothersome, ask the child questions such as, "Why do you think a character behaved a certain way?" "Why do you think" questions almost always push a child to go beyond the concrete or literal meaning of the text. It is also helpful to follow up such questions with curiosity—"Really, what gave you that idea?" or "That's interesting. How did you come up with that conclusion?"

The point is not to turn yourself into a questioning machine with your child, but to try to encourage a type of thought process and a dialogue around what the child is reading. Keeping the questions light and maintaining a tone of curiosity, rather than testing or badgering, would be the goal.

TAKEAWAY POINT

Comprehension really equals thinking. At its best, comprehension is not a regurgitation of facts, but an understanding and an interactive process. Questions help develop this understanding. Encouraging a thought process that pushes for considering or reflecting is ideal.

BRDD: Boy Reading Deficit Disorder

You're a twelve-year-old boy. Let's say you have three hours (or more) to kill. Which would you rather do: entertain your superhero fantasies by killing a gazillion bad guys and perhaps saving the world, or read a book? While I haven't conducted this research study, I would predict that of a sample of say 1000 twelve-year-old boys, 999 would choose saving the world (on video, of course).

While I was a boy—in the log cabin era—I entertained my superhero fantasies by playing outside (I was always Batman). There wasn't all that much going on inside, except when we got involved with very deep comic book reading sessions—*Batman, Superman, Legion of Superheroes,* that sort of thing.

I'm not sure what life would have been like had video games been available to us. I think that even reading comics would have been seen as too slow and not having enough juice to hold our fragile attention spans.

Boys of the modern era have a tough time of it slogging through a book. The sense of slowly letting a book unfold over time is becoming increasingly foreign to their experience—"Wait, it could take me three or more weeks to finish this story? No chance."

I know that the usual answer is you have to find subject matter that will engage their interests and they will connect to reading. I'm not so sure. The distractions are running rampant around their poor brains.

One suggestion is to start early, if you can, with a quiet time in the house that becomes sacred down time—no electronic interferences whatsoever (this means adults too). Steering your child to choose among some Newbery award-winning books as a part of the ritual may excite some dormant part of his psyche.

If this sacred, quiet time becomes a part of the household ritual, then going off and saving the world, at least for that hour to an hour and a half, is something that will have to be put on hold. You may find one way of staving off BRDD.

TAKEAWAY POINT

The deck is stacked against preadolescent and adolescent boys' desire to engage with reading. Quite simply, too many other distractions abound. Creating a sacred, no-electronics, family reading hour allows a good habit to form that becomes a part of the flow of the household. One important point: it is not just the child who takes part; everyone in the house must be unplugged—no Internet, no computer, no texting on cell phones. The unbending rule is no electronics across the board.

Does Your Child Have Curriculum ADHD?

A mom came in the other day to talk about her struggling eight-year-old daughter, Hayley, a third grader. Hayley presented with many of the common concerns—difficulty with decoding, reading fluency, spelling, and writing.

"What has the school done for her?" I asked.

The mom answered, "Well, in kindergarten she got Wilson Fundations. Then in first grade she got Reading Recovery." She continued, "The Reading Recovery teacher went out on maternity leave in April and they gave Hayley support with Harcourt Trophies in her regular class. Now they are talking about SRA for next year or Read 180. I really can't keep up with it all. Why do they jump around so much?"

"Sounds like she may have a case of Curriculum ADHD," I responded.

Curriculum ADHD is characterized by jumping from method to method without ever really giving any of them a chance to take hold. My impression is that there's a lot of Curriculum ADHD going on these days. For struggling readers in particular, the better methods—the ones with good clinical and research support—need to be conducted in a focused manner over a long enough period of time for the skills to be internalized and to take hold.

My question is this: if a child is not given sufficient time with a particular method, how do we know if she is responding to the intervention? Could Curriculum ADHD be contributing to the child's difficulty?

TAKEAWAY POINT

At The Cooper Learning Center in New Jersey where I am the director, we tend not to change methods all that often. We are comfortable with the major approaches that we utilize with the struggling children who come to us. The level of intensity and the amount of time that the child is exposed to a method is what counts. Kids with reading issues (even relatively mild ones) need to be given good methods over a long period of time for them to make a difference. Try not to let your child be a victim of Curriculum ADHD.

There Is No Joy in Educationville for Teaching Reading Has Struck Out

In the teaching of literature, joy, excitement, and enthusiasm should all be conveyed. Without these elements, how will children connect to literature?

From what I have observed and heard from many teachers, the joy of teaching literature is being sucked out of the classroom as schools follow "research-based" scripted methods.

A friend of mine who has over thirty years' experience teaching summed it up. "There's no joy," she said. "There's no excitement. We're being asked to robotically follow scripts. Any deviation is reprimanded and frowned upon by the administration. We have actually been told *not* to read anything, including poetry, to the children that it is not part of the sacred research-based series we are forced to use in the school. Most of the poems in the program aren't even real poems with poets' names attached to them; rather, they are composed by the company. It's very sad. Teaching never used to be like this."

If the title of this chapter sounds familiar to you, you may have been exposed to Earnest Lawrence Thayer's poem, "Casey at the Bat," in school. This is one of America's beloved poems that used to be taught joyfully in the schools. (Funny, I don't remember the teachers using a research-based scripted manual to teach "Casey.")

Mind you, as a psychologist specializing in dyslexia and learning disabilities, I greatly value a bottom-up, skills-based (research supported) approach to teaching children how to decode and read more fluently. Decoding and fluency are skills that contribute to reading, and methods that teach struggling readers these skills have utilitarian value.

However, decoding instruction should not be confused with literature instruction, or with teaching reading in the broadest sense. These methods are *no substitute* for teaching literature. Research should guide instruction and interaction with children, not hold teachers hostage. When the joy is taken out of teaching and the oxygen has left the room, what is left?

Schools should rightfully look to the research evidence to help them make decisions. But removing the teacher's personality, joy, and enthusiasm will lead to boredom and disconnection. Teaching fabricated "literature" robotically will lead to legions of children detesting the reading process.

Good teaching is an art that involves many intangibles. Once these intangibles are devalued, much will be lost. There will be no "joy in Mudville, for mighty Casey will strike out."

TAKEAWAY POINT

The best teaching has always involved conveying joy and excitement. This is even more pronounced with subjects like literature and poetry. As a teacher, you may feel powerless to do anything about having to follow a script, but try to find time in your day to convey joy and excitement to the children. As a parent, if your child is feeling deadened by robotic research-based reading programs, advocate for balance with other types of teaching.

Struggling on the Reading Road: Summary Points

1. The vast majority of children referred for special education or independent evaluations are largely referred because of problems with reading (i.e., decoding and reading fluency).
2. Indicators that appear as early as four or five years of age can suggest a child will have difficulty with the early development of reading skills. These indicators do not immediately suggest disability, but they predict later difficulty.
3. There is no gain in waiting once you have identified some of the cracks (indicators).
4. Screenings do not have to be very involved (or expensive) assessments, but you need to have them done by a professional who knows what he is identifying (e.g., phonemic awareness, decoding, reading fluency).
5. Understanding each of the stages of reading development provides you with a road map at any given time for what

your child needs and what your instructional emphasis should be.

6. Don't scattershot your remediation. Target a specific area (e.g., decoding, vocabulary, or comprehension, to name a few) and employ structured methodologies that have been shown by research and good clinical practice to be effective.

7. If your child is in Stages I and II of development, then there is still work that is needed with decoding and reading fluency. This type of work should be your primary emphasis while she is still in these stages.

8. Beyond Stages I and II, the emphasis should be on the range of comprehension skills and written expression. These skills include developing higher-order reasoning, forming inferences, drawing conclusions, and generating predictions, among others.

9. Be mindful of the three major instructional levels (i.e., independent, instructional, frustration). Be especially attuned to whether your child is operating in waters that he can't handle. If that is the case, the teacher must be informed.

10. Research helps guide education but, unfortunately, it seems that much of the joy of learning is being supplanted by robotic teaching approaches. Keep advocating through the principal and the school board to challenge this style of teaching as it will not encourage children to be connected to the reading process.

PART TWO

Struggling on the School Road (ADHD and Other Related Issues)

Kids on the rockier road often have a combination of ADHD issues and a variety of other learning problems. Sometimes it is difficult to put these children squarely in one category or another. It can be challenging for parents to know the appropriate direction to go in when dealing with issues of medication and classification. School issues can impact families tremendously. A mom said to me some time ago, "School is all we ever argue about at home." A dance frequently takes place between spouses that involves "You're too soft" and "No, you're too hard" finger-pointing.

So many children fall into a zone where they are struggling, yet apparently not badly enough to warrant receiving any remedial services. What do we do with these children, who are, in fact, floundering? Many children are ineligible for services, such as special education, yet are struggling in what I call the "zone of no zone"—the low end of the average range. Children who fall in this area (as do many of the kids I see) will struggle without such support. What then?

Schools are under siege from so many different directions. At the time of the writing of this book, massive budget cuts were taking place in practically every state in the country. Sometimes, though, budgets are not the whole issue, as evidenced by the willingness of some schools to be creative and innovative.

As I did in *The Shut-Down Learner*, I still maintain that the relationship with a teacher and the encouragement a child receives from that teacher makes a world of difference. In an era of believing that test scores will reveal all, there is another side to education that is often unspoken or currently out of favor, and that is the intangible quality of a relationship between a teacher and a child. There can be power and magic in that relationship. If we don't keep that connection, legions of children will be lost.

In the mid-1990s ADHD awareness exploded onto the educational scene. Prior to this time there was little discussion about ADHD (attention deficit hyperactivity disorder). Neurologists, psychiatrists, and other medical professionals were not that much a part of the school landscape.

I have always bristled at the perspective that ADHD is the sole reason that children struggle in school. This approach seems too reductionist to me, too simplistic. I also think that the message the parent receives—once "the diagnosis" is given—often results in a sense that the case is now closed, and medication is the only answer.

My experience with almost all the struggling kids I've met over the years is that the issues are much more complex than many professionals care to admit. Yes, medication can play an important role in helping the child, but parents understandably have lots of concerns with this approach, and their concerns need to be acknowledged and handled sensitively. Putting a child on medication is an enormous leap of faith for many parents, and is often accompanied by a great deal of skepticism that needs to be addressed.

With that said, I have also witnessed children being helped enormously by sensible medical treatments, and in the context of a broader-based assessment, when other issues are considered and understood (such as reading, learning, and social issues), I am more positively inclined to support the recommendation.

Physicians need to understand that their view, which I have heard repeatedly, "I (the physician) will address the attention issue, and let the school evaluate the child for educational issues," may not be helpful. Too often the child does not meet any of the criteria for receiving special services. There are many children who are struggling, yet not severely enough to warrant a special-education evaluation, let alone reach the standard to be classified, once evaluated. For these children it is often the case that medication is the only answer the parents are given. I think this is unfortunate.

The following chapters touch on some of these complexities. There are no easy answers to these issues, but I am hoping these will help you gain some perspective and direction.

School can be a very demanding place, especially for children who are not traveling on the smooth road. While everyone has some type of neurological variability that challenges them in some area, kids with learning disabilities face daily challenges in school that often expose them, opening them up to embarrassment and a sense of shame.

One of the biggest issues that these kids face is being given tasks that are simply over their heads. I tend to look at learning problems as a juncture between the child's capacity to meet the task demands and the task itself. Think of an uncoordinated child being asked to get up and swing a baseball bat at a Little League game. Every once in a while he may get a hit, but striking out and making out after out is the more common experience. The child's developmental ability and skill in hitting a baseball simply aren't there. Perhaps there are exercises that could be done at lower levels (e.g., practicing on a stationary tee, softer tosses, etc.) to allow the child to develop a greater level of confidence and mastery.

The same thinking applies to children with learning disabilities.

As a general rule, I feel that we need to look at the task being given, and if it is over the child's head, we have to back up and make it simpler, more digestible. Sure, trying harder (a frequent request from parents and teachers) may help some, but over time this wears the child down and cannot be sustained. It is up to us, as adults, to examine what we are asking the child to do and see if the task truly falls within the child's zone of competence. Certainly some struggling to accomplish a given task is fine, but how much struggling is acceptable and when does struggling become overwhelmingly frustrating?

We must take our cues from the child. Operating in frustration does no one any good.

Step Right Up, Folks!

Step right up folks! Our unproven, unsubstantiated therapy and treatment is guaranteed to cure all the things that bother you about your child. That's right—for this low fee, a special offer of $3,499 over the next year, we will cure bedwetting, ADHD, reading disabilities, and plain old child orneriness!! All you have to do is plunk down your money (10 percent discount for cash up front), bring in your child for special treatment twice a week for a year, and you will see amazing results in the child. But wait, there's more: When you sign your child up for therapy, this nutrio-supplement can be yours for a whopping 60 percent off the regular retail price ($199)!! This supplement will get your child to stop bothering you at the dinner table and in restaurants. It might even cure sibling rivalry! That's right, folks. Step right up!!!

It seems that every five years or so a hot new treatment bursts onto the market that is guaranteed to cure ADHD, dyslexia, behavior issues, and other child issues of concern. I have known parents to spend thousands of dollars for questionable, unproven therapies only to have the child left in the same position he was in when the therapy started.

Many such therapies make no sense and are supported by little legitimate research, or by "research" that was conducted primarily by the person or company trying to sell the product. In addition, these methods often address the problem indirectly.

For example, if you want your child to learn to read better, then target reading with sensible approaches that have been field-tested. Don't seek alternative, roundabout means of developing reading skills; there are no vitamin supplements or balance-beam exercises that will develop phonics or reading fluency. If focus and attention in class are your concerns, then these should be addressed directly.

Before you try to cure "all things child," be very careful. Don't be so quick to sign up for the cure!

TAKEAWAY POINT

Be wary of expensive treatments that have not been independently researched or field-tested. Make sure that you are clear on which area you are targeting with your interventions and treatments. More often than not, quick treatments that promise too much are probably good at one thing only: taking your money. There are a number of websites that can offer commentary on what is supported in the research. (See Appendix.)

The Blind Men and the Elephant
(Dissecting Childhood)

It was six men of Indostan
To learning much inclined,
Who went to see the Elephant
Though all of them were blind,
That each by observation
Might satisfy his mind.

The above quote comes from the parable of the Blind Men and the Elephant. A group of blind men (or men in the dark) touch an elephant to learn what it is like. Each one touches a different part—but only one part—such as trunk, tusk, or ear. Of course, each describes the elephant quite differently from their perspective.

Sometimes I feel like we are doing the same with children. Different professionals will identify a certain part of the "elephant" and recommend a treatment from that point of view.

Recently a mom came in to discuss her pleasant but struggling eight-year-old son, Evan, who had seen many professionals since the age of four.

"So, what was recommended?" I ask.

"Since kindergarten we've been on this three-or-so-year mission to help him," the mom said. "He just isn't making progress in reading and the gap is widening. We first saw an OT (occupational therapist) who felt there were sensory issues. She felt Evan should get Interactive Metronome therapy. Then we read about special colored lenses for reading and found a person in New York who specializes in a tinted-lens treatment, which she recommended for Evan. An audiologist then found a central auditory processing disorder and recommended that we go to her office for a year's computer treatment to address the auditory issues. The neurologist we saw wants him on medication for ADHD. Dietary supplements and spinal manipulation were recommended by the chiropractor. Then there was the 'train the brain' program offered at the nearby learning center. I really have no idea what to do and am overwhelmed by all of this. I just want him to learn how to read better."

If reading is the primary concern, then Evan's mother should seek good reading instruction. It's common sense.

To hit a tennis ball better, you wouldn't go for swimming lessons. Why is reading any different? It's a skill that can be taught and practiced.

Maybe dissecting the elephant so much is not that helpful.

TAKEAWAY POINT

Often in this day and age there is a lack of common sense guiding the direction that parents take with their child. Understand that professionals tend to see things from their own window. The more specific the specialty (e.g., auditory, visual), the more narrow the window. Get clear on what you are remediating before you commit a significant amount of time and money.

TRY THIS

If you are seeking treatments from different professionals, make sure you are asking the professional exactly what the goals of the treatment are and how the program can deliver these goals. Make sure you are comfortable with whether your questions are being answered. Be certain that there is a match between your areas of concern and the program being recommended. Does the program pass the common sense test? If it does not, you may want to think twice.

Two Roads

You know what Robert Frost said, "Two roads diverged in a yellow wood…"

Continuing the metaphor of two roads, about 50-60 percent of the population has a relatively smooth ride when it comes to school. Sure, there are some pebbles, rocks, and a few potholes in the road, but with the big items—academic and social functioning—the kids on this road get a relatively smooth ride.

Then there are the other kids. These kids travel down a bumpy road filled with potholes. For a whole host of co-mingling variables it's not an easy ride for them.

Children aren't broken. They don't need fixing.

What we can do is make their bumpy road a little smoother.

Smoothing the road a bit can take many forms. A lot of it is turning down the heat and curbing all the yelling and teeth gnashing related to school.

Maybe tonight, instead of all the homework stress, play a game of Uno. Maybe your child likes drawing or building a Lego model. If your kid is older, have her play you some music that she's been listening to on her iPod (that you have no idea about). How about you go for a walk together?

Let the child take the lead.

One rule, though: you're not allowed to bring up school during that time. You're just trying to smooth the road a bit, one pothole at a time.

TAKEAWAY POINT

If your child is on the rough road, it's not always about homework and schoolwork. Find ways to help smooth the road for him; he's hurting and needs support.

TRY THIS

Set aside a no-electronics time period for about an hour, once a week on average. Pull out some board games, card games like Uno, or some type of arts and crafts activities to do with your child. During this time period there is no talking at all about school. Just enjoy the activity.

Doing the ADHD Dance

While there's no magic cure or one-size-fits-all solution for ADHD, it's first important to try to sort out the different variables that may seem like ADHD, but may be representative of other issues. This type of assessment approach takes some time. Sometimes professionals are too quick to diagnose, without seeing the bigger picture, as you'll see here.

A mom came in to talk to me about her six-year-old twin child, Jonathan. Born prematurely after an emergency caesarian section, Jonathan was starting to display a variety of difficulties in mastering early learning concepts, such as letter naming, sound awareness, and other basic skills. In addition to this, he was the type of child who tended to show confusion when engaged with simple language tasks.

An example of this was Jonathan's response when a teacher asked the children to name their favorite holiday activity with their family. Jonathan answered, "A Lego Star Wars."

Clearly, Jonathan was confused.

As I inspected Jonathan's earlier assessment, it became clear to me that he had a range of difficulty with tasks that involved retrieving words, labeling, and understanding "what" and "why" questions. His profile suggested red flags that would contribute to a whole package of difficulty with learning tasks in the early grades and beyond.

At some point in the discussion, the mom showed real frustration when she recounted a one-time (half hour) session that she'd had with a neurologist who saw Jonathan when he was four-and-a-half years of age.

"Can you imagine," she started, exasperated, "after twenty minutes of talking to me and just five minutes with Jonathan, the physician labeled him ADHD and suggested we put him on medication. He was only four!"

I understood her frustration. Here was a boy who possessed all the indicators that learning was going to be tough going, largely because of the complications with his weak language and fine-motor functions. Yet the physician conveyed the simplistic explanation of ADHD and prescribed medication as the "cure." (At least that's what the mom took away from the session.)

This was the wrong message at the wrong time. And more importantly, Jonathan actually needed a broad assessment of his key language and fine-motor functions so that specific and targeted interventions could follow.

It was the wrong time to start the ADHD dance.

TAKEAWAY POINT

Even if your child's been labeled as having ADHD, be on your guard against simplistic explanations that do not take into account a range of other variables. Language functions, for example, are extremely important. Certain types of visual problems can also make it harder to pay attention during reading. Weaknesses in these functions can lead to a great deal of confusion that may look like ADHD. Without a thorough assessment, though, you would never know. Before deciding to put a child on medication, be sure you've checked into other areas of your child's functioning that might explain the off-task behavior or distractibility.

Clogged Fuel Lines

By its nature, school places certain demands on the child throughout the day. Most children typically face a number of tasks that they find challenging and difficult to manage. When faced with such challenges, many will work through their difficulty to arrive at solutions, and thus complete the tasks before them. These are the kids whom I referred to earlier as traveling down the smooth road. They certainly face hurdles but, by and large, have enough reserve in their tank to manage them.

What about the other kids, the ones who seem unable to finish tasks, who are more easily distracted and have trouble dealing with the hurdles?

These kids don't work through their challenges so readily.

One of the biggest concerns facing these kids is the issue of sustained mental effort. Put another way, these kids have "clogged fuel lines" for completing difficult tasks. They simply don't have enough "fuel" to push through their difficulty in managing school tasks.

Take Jenny, age nine. To hear her described, Jenny is an affectionate, loving child who tries to be helpful. At the same time, though, she is quite impulsive and unable to manage tasks that require sustained mental effort.

When I started to work with Jenny, I saw very quickly that she had a clogged fuel line for task difficulty. Just two minutes into a task she'd start whining, "Do we have to do the whole page?" followed by, "I have to go the bathroom." Whenever she faced the slightest difficulty, she'd start rolling around in her chair and repeatedly dropping her pencil on the floor. Jenny had virtually no capacity to manage any frustration or to face the hurdles that she encountered.

Clogged fuel lines present no easy solutions. Medication can be helpful, as stimulant medication can provide a certain amount of mental energy. However, many parents are reluctant to go that route, especially early on in the process when the child is still very young.

Trying to provide enough structure and incentive may also be helpful. Acknowledging the child's feelings about the task can also reduce some of the growing emotional resistance and tension. For example, at home you might say something like, "Jenny, I know you hate this activity, and I see it's hard, but I'd like you to give it a shot. I'll set this clock. We won't do more than fifteen minutes." This type of conversation that acknowledges the difficulty can come across as enormously supportive to the child, in great contrast to the usual anger-tinged interactions.

Ultimately, a certain amount of realism is required. Knowing the nature of your kid and understanding that a clogged fuel line is part of the child's make-up is better than getting upset with her. Try working in small steps, increasing the level of difficulty a little at a time, and keep the teacher in the loop as to what you are trying to accomplish, so the teacher is on board. Circumventing the assignment of frustration-level work to your child is enormously helpful.

TAKEAWAY POINT

Conceptualizing your child as having a clogged fuel line may help to take some of the edge and strain out of your interaction. Such kids need a lot of patient understanding, along with good structure and guidance. Be realistic, and understand your child's tendencies.

TRY THIS

Medication is often the most direct and quickest route to address clogged fuel lines. However, even if the child responds well to the medication, there will be large periods of time (typically into the evening) where the medication will have little to no effect. That is why you always need to be thinking about a combination of the non-medical approaches to bring to the situation. Breaking tasks down into smaller chunks is helpful. Kids also respond to acknowledgement. "You will earn a marble (or big green check on the calendar) if you give me twenty good minutes without any whining or complaining. When we get ten marbles (or checks) you get to pick out your favorite ice cream sundae treat or get to stay up a half hour later on Friday night (something like that)."

The key is to try to keep it positive and not have the whole scene deteriorate into a screaming match.

— —

Age-Adjustment Strategy

When I got my first job as a psychologist at the Hill Top Preparatory School—a school for adolescent children with learning disabilities in the Philadelphia suburbs—the director of the program, Dr. Elissa Fisher, offered a caution to her staff that has always stayed with me. She reminded us that when talking to the children at the school, it is essential to set aside their real age and to view them instead as being much younger than that in their maturity level.

So, when talking to a fifteen-year-old, for example, the usual assumptions about emerging teen issues may not necessarily apply. In effect, it was better to think of the child as approximately a third younger than their real age (around eleven years old, in this case), in their social and emotional development.

Many years later while I was attending a conference on ADHD, Dr. Russell Barkley, the renowned ADHD researcher, made the same basic point concerning ADHD children. He noted that among the top things on the list of "what to do" with ADHD children is to view them as being younger than their actual age.

When parents come in, frustrated by all of the things that the child is doing or is not doing, they usually make comments along these lines:

- He's not responsible.
- She doesn't follow directions.
- When will he ever learn? He's fifteen!

I try to encourage patience and understanding, and to help the parents see that so many of these children are on a different timetable.

I can tell you this. Years later, many of those kids that I knew as teenagers back in Hill Top have contacted me just to check in and say "hello." To a person, I am impressed with how they've grown into mature adults. The three-year gap between their real age and their maturity level that may have been quite pronounced back in high school just doesn't matter anymore.

So, parents of LD (learning disabled) and ADHD children, take a few years off your child's age and with this age-adjustment strategy your list of what he "should" be doing will also be adjusted.

TAKEAWAY POINT

If your child has ADHD or LD (or both), watch out for statements such as, "He's fifteen, he should be able to manage this by himself," or any variation on that theme. Looking at your child with an age-adjustment mentality will help reduce tension. Your adjustment will be closer to the reality, not an arbitrary timetable of what a child "should" be like at a certain age.

ADD (Attention Deficit Disorder) = BDD (Boredom Deficit Disorder)

Imagine you're a twelve-year-old child sitting in your middle-school class. The teacher hands out what's possibly the third or fourth worksheet you've received that day. You're a dutiful type, but even so, you basically want to run out of the room screaming from boredom. But you know that if you start acting out you'll get in trouble, the teacher will call your parents, and no good will come of it. So you tolerate the horribly boring class and complete the worksheet. It's not that you like the tedium and boredom brought on by yet another worksheet, but the voice in your head convinces you to keep a lid on your boredom. You don't want to get into any trouble with the teacher or your parents.

Not so, the person sitting next to you—Aiden.

Aiden's literally crawling out of his skin. He starts complaining to the teacher, who is getting irritated with him. He keeps dropping his pen on the floor and tilting his chair back, and you think to yourself, "Oh no, Aiden's not going to fall out of his seat again, is he? Isn't he on that medication or something? I think I heard my mom whisper something about that. It doesn't look like it's working."

Then the teacher tells Aiden that since he didn't finish the sheet, he will have to stay in during recess or take it home and finish it as homework. Aiden just slumps over.

"Why couldn't Aiden just have done it like everyone else?" you wonder.

You think to yourself, you're glad you're not like Aiden. You can finish the stupid worksheet. You can deal with the boredom, even though you don't want to.

TAKEAWAY POINT

One of the fundamental traits of ADHD-style children is their profound difficulty in managing boredom. No one likes to sit in boring classes or lectures, but some children have the ability to tough it out, while ADHD-style children do not. They pull the "rip cord" much faster, trying to escape what they perceive to be intolerable. So be careful as a teacher not to over-worksheet the children. Ask yourself, "Is the work fair? Is it tedious?" Sometimes it's hard to answer these questions, but even just thinking about them may offer insight into how the material is received.

ADHD Kryptonite: Lunchroom and Playground

Scene 1: The Lunch Room – Jack's Brain

"Gee, it's so wild and noisy in here. Everybody's throwing stuff. Ha ha! Max is so good at putting food in his nose. Maybe I'll try that, too!

"Why is that lunch lady getting mad at me? Max was putting food in his nose first; how come she didn't see that? Max never gets yelled at. Now she wants me to sit off by myself until we go outside. It's not fair. I was just having fun—just like Max."

Scene 2: The Playground – Jack's Brain

"Cool...we're outside...great to be out....I'm so sick of being inside...oh man...I can't wait to go over to the slide area and swing down...oh, man...there's a line...oh, there's Max, maybe I can jump in front of him...wait, there's a cool stick that I can throw over the fence...wow, that went pretty far...better than yesterday's stick.

"Oh, no, that lunch lady is coming over to me again and she's got that look...

"I didn't mean to throw the stick," I tell her.

"Phew. She lets me go this time. Back to the swing...cool there's Max. We can jump down together....oh, man it's lineup time already...how come the line teacher is yelling at me? I didn't push in line, did I? Everyone else was doing it, too..."

Scene 3: The Classroom – Jack's Brain

"Oh, man. The teacher is filling out that daily report card thing... that stinks...I got another frowny face on the report card for lunch and playground. I'm going to get yelled at and punished again.

"I didn't even do anything…How come Max never gets in trouble?"

TAKEAWAY POINT

Traveling inside the head of an ADHD-style boy would certainly be a thrill ride. There isn't all that much reflecting or considering of consequences. You can easily see how school can be a challenge for a kid like Jack.

Playing the Odds:
Which Horse Would You Bet?

Having been raised by a father who enjoyed playing the horses, I am well acquainted with how the odds work.

But don't worry. I'm not going to tell you how to win at the track, but rather how to change the odds in your favor.

Kids rarely think about changing the odds in school, yet they should. They need to be schooled in odds. Take the conversation I had with Forrest, a very sincere twenty-year-old junior in college. Among other things, Forrest told me how hard it was for him to pay attention when he was in the lecture hall.

"I don't know why—I just tune out," Forrest said. "I've always had trouble with lectures."

"Let me guess," I said to him. "When you arrive at the lecture hall, you're not thinking about much, right? You kind of just land wherever you land in the class. Then, about ten minutes into the lecture, you pull out your cell phone and check the Internet. About fifteen minutes or so into the lecture, you start texting your friends. By twenty minutes in you have no written notes, no idea what's going on, and are dying to get out of the class. Is that your experience?"

Forrest grinned widely, thinking perhaps that I was some kind of prescient mind reader.

I said to him, "Seriously, would you bet on that horse?"

He shook his head, and I could tell he knew exactly what I meant.

"So, Forrest," I continued, "Let's look at a different horse— let's change the odds. Maybe there are little things you could do to tip the odds in your favor. For example, one thing you might want to do is sit closer to the teacher. Just changing your position in class may help you pay attention."

I went on, "How about trying to make some pictures on the right side of the page of what is being discussed in class along with some written notes? That might help you get more connected." I knew that Forrest liked drawing, and having some visual reference points would help him later with his recall.

"Let's also say you forced yourself to jot down at least five questions that came up from the teacher's lecture. These questions would be ones that you predict might occur later on a test. Forming questions might help you be a more active listener."

I could see that Forrest was thinking about these possibilities.

"Now compare horse A to horse B above," I suggested. "Which one would you pick?"

Forrest got the message immediately and seemed excited to try a couple of the suggestions.

Helping Forrest see that he could improve his odds was a good first step. It will take a long time for him to fully buy in, but you have to start somewhere. At least he was thinking about the odds, something he had never done previously.

Now, off to the races!

TAKEAWAY POINT

Try to help your child, especially a somewhat older child, to start considering the odds of success, relative to school, given one approach style compared to another. Helping him to think about "tilting the odds" in his favor may make a difference. It really comes down to a passive versus an active approach. Helping people with ADHD and other related learning problems to be more mindful of their approach and overcome the passive tendencies is beneficial.

Common Sense and Reasonable 504 Plans

Many parents come to me with reports from a variety of other professionals, containing ten, twenty, or even thirty boilerplate recommendations to be incorporated in the child's 504 Plan. Usually my eyes start to glaze over after reading past canned recommendation number five or so.

What do you think is happening to the teacher when she looks at these recommendations? Right—glazed over eyes. It's a prescription for doing none of the accommodations.

Even though you feel very armed and ready with your doctor's multiple recommendations, the fact is the school will not be able to do a vast majority of what is being suggested.

Contrary to what many seem to believe, 504 Plans are not school-created services. We have come to think of the 504 Plan erroneously as being synonymous with providing services for ADHD.

In fact, 504 Plans come out of the Americans With Disability Act (ADA), and a range of different disabilities falls under them.

They are intended to help level the field by providing accommodations that would help put the disabled person on more even ground.

For example, ADHD-style people have trouble following directions. Therefore, a simple accommodation would be that the teacher goes over to the child to check in after she has started the class on an activity. Theoretically, this helps level the playing field by aiding someone who has trouble following directions, compared to those who seem capable. This seems to be straightforward enough, with a healthy dose of common sense.

Another necessary accommodation would be for children who show "sluggish cognitive tempos," which is common among kids who are significantly inattentive. Their internal clock speed is simply not very rapid. As I like to explain it to the child, "I don't think you are going to be an emergency-room doctor one day."

Someone with a sluggish tempo will probably need some type of support and accommodation in the classroom. A good teacher will take the child off to the side and say something like, "Frank, I know you get nervous taking tests because you are on the first few items when everyone else is finishing up. Not to worry. We will work it out."

Again, common sense prevails and the child is reassured through this accommodation.

When creating 504 Plans, try to get in touch with your Inner Common Sense. Let this guide you in creating a few sensible and helpful accommodations.

My advice would be that you simplify things. Come up with two or three (at the most) really useful things that you think your child's teacher can do to help your child along. Come up with reasonable accommodations that help to make the road a little smoother for your child.

For anything beyond three recommendations, the school will just be checking off boxes on a 504 template for you to sign and for the school to ignore, until the time that the 504 is to be revisited a year later for signing and ignoring.

And one more thing: insist that the school put the 504 accommodations into sentences rather than some existing checklist. An individually tailored plan is far better than a standard template.

TAKEAWAY POINT

504 Plans are accommodations for a range of people with disabilities. The idea is that the accommodation should help level the playing field for the handicapped individual. Be reasonable and let common sense guide you. Don't accept formulaic checklist 504 Plans. The plan should be written individually for your child.

With 504 Plans there's a tendency to overwhelm schools with requests being made by outside professionals. Many reports written by these professionals have boilerplate 504 accommodations that are not necessarily written with your own child's individual needs in mind. Ask yourself, in consultation with your professional, what would be the small handful of accommodations that could prove to be helpful to your child?

TRY THIS

In a quiet moment reflect on your child's needs and write down three or four basic accommodations that you think could be helpful to your child. Keep in mind that there are usually a good twenty or so other children in the class, so by trying to do too much, the accommodations that could really matter will be forgotten. Usually, ADHD-style children need help with understanding directions and staying on track when they get bored or frustrated. Focusing on accommodations like that may help with these essentials. Put your accommodations down in plain language. Don't ask for the moon and the stars, as this will only lead to adversarial relations with the school.

Killing the Rainforest One IEP at a Time

There's nothing worse than when parents come in to my office to consult with me and they bring those thick folders loaded with one IEP (Individualized Education Plan) after another. I know I have some kind of comprehension problem because, after all of these years, whenever I start to read the IEPs my attention wanders and I can't understand them.

When I was a young special education teacher, IEPs were supposed to be liberating for those with handicaps. The intention of the law, as I recall, was that a plan would be drawn up and individualized for each child.

I didn't think it was supposed to be a template of items to be checked off a list, with page after page of checklists that do not seem to capture the essence of the child's disability or what she really needs.

I would rather have a one-page IEP that said something like:

- By the end of the year, the goal is that Sarah's decoding skills will show improvement in word patterns that are one syllable with short vowel sounds (e.g., *clip, chop, lunch, test*).
- By the end of the year, Sarah will demonstrate that she understands how to write complete sentences with at least one adverb and one adjective.
- By the end of the year, Sarah will be able to read a second-grade-level story aloud and demonstrate 98 percent word mastery within a two-minute selection.

Wouldn't three specifically targeted goals be better than twenty-odd pages of checklists?

I know, I'm dreaming.

We would save some trees in the rainforest, though.

TAKEAWAY POINT

I understand that IEPs have evolved into being the long legal documents that they are today. Try to push the special education team into writing down goals in straightforward language that is clearly articulated. What specifically are they proposing to achieve with your child? For example, "By the end of the school year John will show a 90 percent mastery of one-syllable words that have short vowel sounds." That seems pretty straightforward and understandable, doesn't it?

Winning the Battle but Losing the War

Sometimes parents are living in Dreamy-Dream Land when it comes to accommodations and 504 Plans. They come up with all these schemes and interventions that may make some sense on paper (although often they don't), but in reality the child wants no part of the accommodations and is not interested in the schemes.

If you are not around many kids (other than your own), you may have forgotten the number one law in the universe of childhood—"Don't do anything that will embarrass me or make me look different." Now, parents may not like that law and we may do some teeth gnashing about it, but it is an immutable law.

So, for example, if your child is the one who has some blinking device on his desk to cue him in to pay attention at different intervals, you may be winning a battle (paying attention better), but losing a war (experiencing shame and embarrassment). Maybe it's not worth it.

Most of us experienced shame at some point in our schooling. Many experienced it far too often. You can probably remember, like it was yesterday, when you heard snickers from others who made fun of you for something you did. So when you are drawing up your elaborate 504 Plans, put yourself in your child's shoes before you do battle with the school. Maybe the child's core feeling is, "Thanks, Mom, but no thanks."

TAKEAWAY POINT

Sometimes interventions or accommodations look good on paper or make sense to an adult, but to a child they lead to feelings of discomfort, shame, and embarrassment. Before implementing any intervention or accommodation, be sure to check what impact it will have on the child's emotional well-being.

Should a Child Be on Medication While Being Evaluated?

What about kids who are already on medication when it comes to further evaluation? I've been asked about the pros and cons of having a child on medication while being tested:

> Please address whether a child should be on medication while he's being assessed for executive function issues. Some of the specialists we refer to around the country say to lower the medication when testing so you see the real child. Others say give the meds so you can see the potential. What do you think?

This question comes up a lot for me. Before bringing their child in for an assessment, parents will often ask, "Should I keep her on medication for the testing?"

Like most things in this business, there isn't a clear-cut answer. (That's why my hair turns progressively gray with each passing day.)

To me, the question is best answered by another question: "What's your purpose in doing the assessment?"

For example, let's say your child has had a year of tutoring (while on medication) and you want to know how the child is progressing. In that scenario, having the child on medication during the assessment makes sense.

But if your purpose is to get a second opinion as to whether the child still needs to be on medication, then it probably makes sense for the psychologist to see the child off of her medication, to get a better feel for the child. (Mind you, with this question I am making reference only to stimulant-type medication, such as Adderall or Concerta, since stimulants are short-acting and are in and out of the system quickly.)

Bottom line: get clear on your purpose for doing the assessment, and this will help to resolve the question of whether to medicate or not during the evaluation.

TAKEAWAY POINT

The question of whether to keep the child on medication during the assessment is not easily answered. Getting clear on your reason for the assessment will help to guide the clinician as to the type and nature of the assessment to be conducted.

Going Columbo

It was a sad day recently when Lieutenant Columbo (Peter Falk) of the famed TV show from the 1970s died. Little did Mr. Falk know what a central part his character has played over the years in my advising parents how to approach school meetings.

Here's how "Going Columbo" works. Parents have lots of questions and concerns about what they are being told. Instead of coming across as too confrontational, I encourage parents to start sounding really perplexed, just like Columbo did (even though he already had the whole case nailed).

Body language is crucial when Going Columbo. Scratching your head a lot and looking confused are essential. You can't be afraid to sound dumb, and always have to use the phrase, "There's just one more thing...."

For example, a parent might say something like, "I know I get confused" (while scratching head a lot) "but it says here that his vocabulary score is in the 9th percentile. Like, is that a good score?" (Squint and tilt head.) "It doesn't sound very good, but I may not get it...help me out...I know I'm grasping at straws, but wouldn't that vocabulary score affect something, like maybe comprehension?" (Keep scratching your head, looking dumber and dumber.)

"And wait, there's just one more thing. I'm confused again. What does percentile mean? I think I remember something about it in a college course. So when you tell me he's 'average' and he's in the 25th percentile, like that's not a great place to be, right? Because if I were in a race that would mean 75 percent of the people would be ahead of me, or do I have that confused?

That doesn't sound very good, does it? I took college a long time ago and I could be forgetting, so please fill me in."

So, before you go in for your next IEP or 504 meeting, practice Going Columbo in front of the mirror. Say little, but scratch your head a whole lot. You'd be surprised how effective it can be. Ask the school to help you out of your confusion, and use the phrase, "Just one more thing."

Get very dumb and ask great questions.

Rest in peace, Lieutenant Columbo!

TAKEAWAY POINT

Lieutenant Columbo had a style of disarming people by appearing confused and befuddled. So parents, rather than approaching school meetings in an overly confrontational or direct manner, try Going Columbo. Ask for clarification to get you through any confusion. Don't be afraid to practice phrases such as, "Just one more thing."

The Zone of No Zone

So many kids who are struggling fall into what I refer to as the "zone of no zone." This is where everyone throws their hands up and says, "Well, your child is in the average range and therefore she is ineligible for service. There's nothing we can do about it."

Eligibility for service, unfortunately, is the driving force behind most special education assessments. I understand that state special education code requires this, but parents get confused when they hear this conclusion that their child is in the "average range." The impression they get is that there are no problems, yet that's hard to reconcile when they see their child struggling daily.

Well, the 30th percentile places you in the lower portion of the average range. This means that 70 percent of the population is ahead of you. It is not comforting to know that you are in the lower portion of the average range and ineligible for service.

When a child is in the lower portion of the average range in reading, spelling, and writing, that's a problem and it needs attention. There are very few children in this range who are reading comfortably and efficiently. For them, reading is a laborious chore.

I think if we were more honest about it, schools would say something along the following lines, which is a different message than the one the parents hear:

> When you are classified for special education, it means your child has a handicap or a disability. In our estimation, your child's issues aren't severe enough to warrant viewing him as handicapped, but we do see him struggling with decoding. Therefore we are going to give him attention every day in a small group with a reading teacher who will practice his decoding skills with him.

Why must a child be handicapped to have someone practice decoding with him? Struggling is struggling, and school is supposed to be about helping kids to overcome their weaknesses.

TAKEAWAY POINT

If your child has been assessed for special education and has been found to be "ineligible for services," that does not mean that there are no needs. Eligibility for a learning disability typically refers to a level of severity that determines disability. Your child may still be struggling in core areas and need attention, even if the school does not deem the child to be eligible to receive services.

Inside the Head of a Boy with a Learning Disability!

Ever wonder what really goes on inside the head of a child who is struggling in school? Take a closer look:

You're a ten-year-old boy with a learning disability. This learning disability stuff is very tough. Every day you look around the room and see people finishing tasks quickly, getting smiles from the teacher for all the work they handed in on time. You don't get those smiles. Writing is particularly galling to you, because you just don't get it—it's so hard. When the teacher starts off the day saying, "Now take out your journals," you just want to run away.

You don't know how to get started in your journal. The teacher says to "Just write what you feel," but you have no idea how you feel. The words on the page bleed into one another. No one can read it. Not even you. Meghan sitting next to you keeps making those stupid snickering faces.

Not only is your writing messy, but it all takes so long. Meghan was completely done before you even had down one sentence (a bad one at that). Worse, the essays go on the bulletin board and the parents are coming in soon and will see all of these. The last paper you handed in was such a mess. You can't stand to see your writing up on the board. "Why do they have to put that junk up on the board?" you wonder. Meghan is getting so annoying.

At home you overheard a bit of tension between your parents. You think you heard your mother saying to your dad, "But he has a 504 Plan" and, "He can take as much time as he likes. Why can't he just get it done?" You really can't stand any of this talk.

You think to yourself, "What is this 504 Plan anyway? I wonder if it has anything to do with those wires the doctor put on my head a few weeks ago to test my brain waves?"

That visit did nothing to help your self-esteem. Wires on your head? Brain waves? Yeesh! You repeat their words to yourself, "Take as much time as I like!! Who wants more time?? I hate writing. I don't want to take more than one minute for journal. Are they kidding me?"

You know what's going to happen. You'll have to do it tonight if you can't finish. "I can't stand Meghan. She's already on the worksheet and I haven't even started the journal. 504 Plan?? They want me to take twice as long to do a bad job. I'd like to see them spend hours on something only to get a grade of a D or an F."

Well, tomorrow's another day.

TAKEAWAY POINT

It is really tough sledding if you are in an elementary class and you don't have the requisite skills to handle all that is being asked of you. Just asking kids to do more of the same can be very frustrating. While they may not be verbalizing all of their feelings, you can bet they are experiencing strong feelings. As tough as it is for a parent to do, try to back up and be patient and supportive when you see your child struggling.

Go to a Carpenter, You Get a Nail

What a crazy business this is, working with struggling children. So much depends on whose office the child lands in. Unlike dentistry, where I imagine there would be a reasonable agreement as to what the problem is and how to fix it, addressing problems related to school struggling is much murkier.

Let's say the problem is a sense that the child is not finishing tasks and is avoiding complex reading activities.

If you went to the audiologist first to check out the child's hearing, chances are the child would be seen as having CAPD or Central Auditory Processing Disorder. Fast ForWord or some other such "train the brain" program may be recommended.

The Occupational Therapist may see sensory issues and suggest a sensory therapy program.

The Neurologist would have his prescription pad out diagnosing ADHD.

The Developmental Optometrist would be recommending vision therapy.

Nutritional experts may be recommending a special diet.

Psychiatrists may be interpreting anxiety and depression as the root issues.

Psychologists and social workers may recommend counseling.

All of these professions can have something to contribute in solving the puzzle of a child's learning problem, and I have referred kids to all of them at one time or another.

Understanding the "go to a carpenter, you get a nail" effect is very powerful. The various professionals who could potentially be involved are not being unsavory (at least most are not), but their recommendations are based on their perspective, that is their professional and personal orientation toward the issues of concern.

Know what you are getting into before taking your child to a specialist. Usually the best first step is to see a professional who functions more like a general practitioner and is capable of considering a variety of "spokes on the wheel," so to speak. For example, a thorough psychoeducational assessment considers all of the different professionals as part of a possible treatment and represents a broad-based (as opposed to a narrower) assessment. There should be no investment in any one treatment. The recommendation that comes out of such an evaluation should steer toward what is in the best interest of the child, not based solely on the treatment offerings of that particular practitioner.

TAKEAWAY POINT

Be wary of starting out with a specific treatment for your child before having a variety of areas considered. Start with a more general approach that considers a number of different areas (e.g., language functions, sensory and perceptual functions, reading, etc.). From such a broad evaluation you can narrow down your treatment options.

The House Looks Fine: What's the Problem?

Many times parents (moms) sense that something is wrong with their child and want to have the child evaluated in school. Once the mom raises the issue, she often hears a version of the following, "Well, she's getting good grades—what's the problem?" As her request for testing is denied, the mom walks away thinking that she was being unduly concerned. She is given the impression that she is over-worrying.

Time goes by. The mom continues to see the child struggle and may seek an outside assessment. More often than not in a situation like this, what I find are "cracks in the foundation" that help to explain some of the struggling and validate the mom's concerns.

These cracks are like the ones in your house. Sure the house looks fine, but the foundation may be a little shaky.

With a child, the shaky foundation doesn't necessarily mean that the child is "disabled," but it also doesn't mean that the child is fine. The good grades may be masking some of the issues of concern (the foundation).

A child can get good grades for all kinds of reasons. For example, a child can probably get a B in most classes in elementary school if she doesn't give the teacher a hard time, hands in her homework, and exhibits other teacher-pleasing behaviors. Many children (especially girls) have figured this out. This approach is a good strategy for not drawing any undue negative attention to yourself. (Boys are notorious for *not* figuring this out.)

Listen to your "mother gut." When you think there are concerns, there usually are. The school may not act on your concerns, but if you are able to do so you should try to have someone check out the foundation.

Ignoring the cracks is never a good policy, whether in your house or with your child.

Cracks widen over time. Problems grow. There is no gain in taking no action.

TAKEAWAY POINT

Even if the school denies a request for assessing your child, if you have concerns you should try to act on them if you can. More often than not the mom's concerns are the result of identifiable "cracks" that need attention. Talk to a psychologist or other learning specialist in your community who understands this concept of identifying cracks and not just labeling a disability.

Help! I'm Being Held Hostage to My IQ

Sometimes I think that we have the notion that before being born all of us lined up in heaven to receive our IQ scores. You can almost imagine hearing the announcement from one of God's helpers, "If you are about to be born, step up so that God can stamp a number in your head. You will carry this number around with you wherever you go on earth. Line up everyone. Get your IQ scores!"

Then as the line proceeds you would hear, "OK, let's see, this one will get a 92—sorry that's the lower portion of the average range…the 32nd percentile…no one will help you. This one gets a 103—well, maybe you'll get help if you need it. You might have enough points. We'll see how bad your reading is though. Uh, oh, here comes a tough one. Woops, sorry you get an 83—that's the 13th percentile. Not likely to be much help for you."

Fast forward to your time on earth. You're a child struggling in school. You don't read very well. Homework is as painful as a toothache. Your parents are irritable with you all the time. In short, you need help. Well, what happens if you have one of those unfortunate numbers stamped in your head?

Essentially this is what your parents are told: "We're sorry, but state regulations are such that there has to be this very large discrepancy between the number that's stamped in your child's brain and the number we calculate to be the reading score. Otherwise, you're just out of luck. Too bad. Next case."

In other words, a child is often held hostage to her IQ.

I see kids like this all the time. It's unfortunate and parents are simply given the wrong message.

Struggling is struggling, no matter what label is given to it. If a child is struggling in fundamental, core areas of reading, spelling, and writing, he needs help and support, regardless of what mythical number is stamped in his brain.

TAKEAWAY POINT

There is probably no concept more misused in education than IQ. The reason it is misused is the overemphasis on the overall score. Most people have a fair degree of variability in their profiles. This variability is crucial. If the school is not offering services to your struggling child, try to advocate for the school to revisit their findings or find other ways to get the child support.

— —

Inclusion: Support in the Deep End of the Pool

If a child is not a good swimmer, yet is in a swimming class taking place in the deep end of the pool, how should this be handled?

I imagine that a swim instructor would have to stay close by, making sure that the child did not go under. (One could question why the child was in the deep end of the pool in the first place, but let's save that for another time.)

For children classified in special education, I often hear that she is receiving inclusion services or is in an inclusion class. Inclusion can take many forms, but it generally means that there is a special-education teacher or assistant in the classroom who plays a secondary, supportive role to the primary teacher. Certain children are assigned to the inclusion teacher and are on her caseload. Typically, she helps these children with the material that they are getting in class. She makes sure the kids are on board, offers pointers, and sees to it that the children are basically keeping up with the class. In other words, the inclusion teacher sees to it that the children who can't handle the deep water do not drown.

I am not knocking inclusion by saying this, but understand that inclusion is the equivalent of the instructor in the deep end of the pool. Inclusion is fundamentally different than direct instruction.

Direct instruction means that specific skills are taught within levels where the child is reasonably comfortable (e.g., the four-foot water, as opposed to the deep end).

If you are the parent of a child who is classified, it is essential that you are clear on the difference. Inclusion is support and drowning prevention, while direct instruction is targeting specific skills to be developed, effectively helping the child become a better swimmer.

Both inclusion support and direct instruction are important, but too often the child only receives one of them.

Without sufficient direct instruction, the child will always need to have someone close by to make sure he does not drown.

TAKEAWAY POINT

While an inclusion class can be very helpful, you need to be very clear on the difference between what is typically received in an inclusion class, in comparison to receiving specialized, direct instruction. Being in an inclusion class and getting special education support is the equivalent to playing a game (e.g., baseball) and getting support to keep you focused and in the game. Direct instruction is directly targeting the skills necessary to play the game.

TRY THIS

If your child is in an inclusion class and is receiving "in-class support," you may want to talk to the teacher about when (or if) your child is receiving direct instruction. In-class support, while helpful, is only one piece of the puzzle.

Old School Concept #3: Task Analysis

The third old school concept, largely forgotten, is "task analysis." With task analysis the idea is that any end-point task that you want someone to master can be broken down into sub-tasks to help the person move along a continuum toward mastery of the skill. Breaking down the steps of a task helps us to understand all of the steps that a child must go through to achieve mastery.

Teaching cognitively impaired children to brush their teeth successfully is the classic example used to illustrate task analysis. Most of us take brushing our teeth for granted, thinking that it's no big deal. We don't tend to consider how many sub-tasks (e.g., taking the cap off the toothpaste, squeezing the tube properly, holding the toothbrush in one hand, etc.) are involved to get to the end point. With cognitively impaired people, however, such a skill may not be so easy to master, and the mastery of the sub-tasks along the way may be of paramount importance to reaching the end point.

Recently a mom talked to me about how her son was struggling in youth football. The usual explanations were offered—he wasn't paying attention or trying hard enough. When I met the child, it became clear to me that there were other explanations. This child was simply too confused and overwhelmed on the field. Sports like football can be quite confusing for a lot of kids. They have trouble with the sequences and the rapid decision-making. (In fact, some time ago I worked with a Division I college football player who could have made it to the pros if he had possessed the ability to keep the play sequences straight.)

Another example of task analysis comes from Zoe, the daughter of a good friend of mine. Zoe, a college student on the autism spectrum, wrote a blog explaining how she needs to create a flow chart to help her successfully leave her room and do all that is necessary to keep the steps straight. Zoe reminds us that patience and understanding are essential, and that we should not take someone's capacity to manage everyday tasks for granted.

My guess is that if we task-analyzed much of what we expect our children to master (like playing football, comprehending a story, making a sandwich, or getting out the door in the morning), we'd see that there are many small steps involved that we may not have considered.

I know my wife is still trying to do that with me in terms of learning how to make the bed properly! Frankly, I don't think she's broken it down enough.

TAKEAWAY POINT

If you see your child struggling with a task, analyze the sub-tasks. Try to break the task down, and then back it up by practicing at easier levels before continuing. This will lead up to mastery of the task.

TRY THIS

Take any task that you can think of, like making a bed, organizing a room, or writing an essay, for example. Analyze what the steps are that lead to the successful completion of the task. Write the steps down in order. This is a good exercise to get you started in task-analysis thinking.

— —

Howard Beale—Where Are You?

Remember the movie *Network,* in which newscaster Howard Beale (played by Noah Finch) is fed up with everything around him and goes on nightly rants Throughout the movie he repeats the phrase, "I'm mad as hell and I'm not going to take it anymore," which becomes his mantra.

I think I am starting to feel like Howard Beale all too often.

One of my rants was triggered by a line in a report on a learning disabled/dyslexic child that said "Frank must learn to accept responsibility for his reading comprehension and to develop his own strategies."

Frank is seven! He's a weak reader! He's not going to accept responsibility for his reading comprehension or develop his own strategies.

(I'm also fed up with the word *strategies,* but that's another rant for another day.)

If Frank were a poor swimmer, would you insist that he swim in the deep end of the pool? Would reminding him to accept responsibility for his poor swimming skills help him along while he floundered?

The answer is self-evident.

Yeesh. I'm mad as hell.

TAKEAWAY POINT

On report cards and assessments there will sometimes be comments such as, "X must learn to take responsibility for _____ (skill)." My inclination is to believe that X can't take responsibility for a skill that he has not yet acquired or mastered. You may want to ask the teacher how a child can take responsibility for a skill that he doesn't yet have. Could you take responsibility for riding a bike if you hadn't learned to ride one yet?

How Do We Fix It?

I spend a good part of my professional life assessing children in an attempt to identify their profiles of strengths and weaknesses. Once a child is assessed, I do my best to explain the data to the parents in straightforward, non-jargon terms. The part of the process I least like is the question that frequently arises: "Well, how do we fix it?"

The reason I don't like this question is that I never know the answer. I never think of kids as needing to be fixed—they're not car engines.

It's better to focus on improving skills rather than "fixing." Skill talk leads to productive understanding which then leads to taking appropriate action steps:

"Oh, I see it's a decoding or reading fluency issue…we can work on those skills."

Or,

"So my child is under too much pressure and we need to yell less, right? OK, we can do that."

Statements of understanding like these imply a next-step action that can lead to improvements.

Children and parents can understand things better when they are put in terms of skills, rather than fixing something (like their brain). For example, rather than saying to the child that he has a disability, which does not lead to a next-step action, focus on the skill that points to a clear direction.

Fixing implies that the child is broken. This is not the message that kids need to hear.

Better questions than, "How do we fix it?" might be, "So, what do we do next?" "What skills are we targeting?"

TAKEAWAY POINT

Even though we currently use the terms *disabled* or *disordered* fairly freely, perhaps the messages that children take from hearing these terms is that something is wrong with them or that they need "fixing." This is not the message I want to give kids. Focusing on specific skills helps the child and the parents get their minds around what to do next.

In the Neck Ache Business

I need to visit the chiropractor.

During much of my professional life, I listen to parents who come in and relate to me the various and sundry things that the school has told them about their child. Hearing some of what the parents are told, I feel my neck twinge. Sometimes I feel it twinge maybe five or six times per one-hour session.

When it's really bad, I sometimes feel like a raccoon in a trap. (Yes, I know, my parents wanted me to go to dental school, but I had to do it my way and chose this career path.)

Just today my neck was twinging a lot, hearing some of the things the mom had been told:

- We really don't know what dyslexia is. (Yes we do.)
- In all my years of teaching, I have never had a dyslexic child in my class, the mom was told by an experienced, second-grade teacher. (Yes, you have. In fact, at any given point you probably had about 20-30 percent of your class on the dyslexic continuum.)
- Spelling really doesn't matter. (Really??)
- The only thing that matters in reading is comprehension. (Is that right? So, when the child sees a word like *porcupine* in the text and reads it as *prickopinny*, that's OK because she got the gist of the story, somehow?)
- Only neurologists and psychiatrists can test for dyslexia, since it is a medical condition. (You mean that a neurologist will give a broad battery of tests to assess dyslexia? Funny, I don't know any in my community who do that.)

On and on it goes.

These quotes were just from a single session with one mom.

I need a heating pad. I'm calling the chiropractor now.

TAKEAWAY POINT

A great deal of misinformation out there is often put forth as fact. Be cautious accepting what you are told and be sure to find reliable professionals to help you sort it out and verify what is being said.

Got the Cure for the Summertime Blues?

Ain't no cure for the summertime blues.
—"Summertime Blues," Eddie Cochran and Jerry Capehart

In the movie *The Tree of Life*—a metaphysical romp depicting the universe's creation from the Big Bang through the dinosaurs to the present day—a good portion of the scenes focused on a family (starring Brad Pitt as the father) in the Midwest sometime around the summer of 1955.

The scenes centering on the family took place mostly through the eyes of the three young boys. One of the striking things was how much these boys played outside, from sunup to sundown, without the hint of adult supervision or interference.

Sure, the kids did some stupid things (or, in the modern parlance, exhibited trouble with "self-regulation" and acted "impulsively"), but then, again, it was summer; they had to get into some trouble. What good would summer be without a little mischief?

In the spirit of summers gone by, try to get the kids outdoors and off their iPad, Wii, Xbox, or whatever other electronic pacifiers they are embracing.

Maybe they can spend a few hours a day without adult steerage.

Maybe they can tromp around in a nearby swamp or pond. (OK, you can put little floaties on them if you are getting nervous.)

Maybe they can dig around in the dirt, roll around in the grass, or catch a few frogs or fireflies in a jar.

Doing some of these "old school" summer activities might just cure a bit of the summertime blues.

TAKEAWAY POINT

Summer is a great time for trying to get kids to go old school. If they spend too much time on their electronic devices, limit it and get them outside.

TRY THIS

With your child, come up with a schedule as to how much time will be acceptable for being on "screens." It's probably better if you enlist their input and come up with a fair schedule that you both are comfortable with.

Screeching on the Violin

Once a pon a time their was a boy who had no friends so he was always alon But then one day every thing change His mom gave him a violin to play it sounded horabel so he said he said I am never playing this agin so then one Day he went in the store and heard a guy play the vialin it sonded awesome so he said to his mom that's how I want to play well then you need to pratis and then he did and he was so good at it.

This is a story written by a ten-year-old boy. It is written in response to a psychological test card that shows a boy looking at a violin. How the character manages the violin and resolves playing the violin in the story created by the child often reveals his or her underlying feelings about achievement and self-worth. This story is written exactly as the boy wrote it.

After working with the boy, I was struck by how much his story presented a true x-ray of how he was feeling. While he knows he is not measuring up—others around him are easily reading chapter books while he struggles at much lower reading levels—he remains optimistic. He also doesn't have too many friends.

This boy needs a connection. He needs to believe in himself more.

He also needs to learn how to write in structured, systematic ways so that he can begin to understand what a sentence is and how to use punctuation. This will take a great deal of time and practice at the sentence level with focused, educational therapy.

If your child is metaphorically screeching on the violin, try to find people who understand and know how to work with kids at both the skill and emotional levels.

TAKEAWAY POINT

Writing can be brutally challenging for many kids. They need direct instruction on how to approach writing, utilizing structured, systematic methods that practice one skill concept at a time until they master it. They also need tremendous support and encouragement.

Open-Ended Writing: A Heavy Load for Many Kids

When I assessed young Michael (age seven and a half), I found him to be extremely bright, with excellent higher-level reasoning skills and a lively, spontaneous personality. Matching his strong cognitive abilities were his reading skills, which were developing nicely.

Yet Michael was having a rough second-grade year. Openly stating how much he disliked school, Michael was becoming discouraged. What was the problem? How could a bright child with good reading skills and a pleasant personality become discouraged so early?

In a nutshell, Michael found writing to be an excruciating process and one that he had to face every morning. For many kids (often the boys), there is a mismatch between their cognitive abilities and their ability to get the words out of their head and onto the page.

For the kids that we are concerned about, those who struggle on the left side of the curve in so many areas, there is probably no school-based task that causes more anguish than writing, in particular open-ended writing.

With open-ended writing, the child is given some kind of prompt, whether in picture form or in a verbal statement, to stimulate the writing. Classic prompts, such as "Write about your weekend," or "Write about the school trip," are open-ended and can be responded to with infinite variation.

Open-ended writing is probably the single most used vehicle in school for developing kids' writing skills. As I understand it, the theory is that the more one does a task (like writing), the better one will become in the skill. This sounds plausible, and for about 60 percent of the school population, this theory probably works pretty well. For the remaining 40 percent though, just doing more of it is problematic.

Open-ended writing places an emphasis on active working memory, the memory that underlies most learning disabilities. To illustrate this emphasis, think about how many mental processes go into the task, "Write about your weekend." You have to:

- Picture the weekend (mental imagery).
- Make decisions about what to choose (weighing importance).
- Organize ideas in a logical order (mental sequencing).
- Find appropriate words and put these in an order (semantic ordering).
- Keep spelling in mind (even if the teacher said not to worry about spelling).
- Distinguish between fragmented and complete sentences.

The list can go on for about twenty more variables that are used in the process of writing. For kids who show weaknesses with active working memory (see WISC-IV profile for a clue about this), all of these variables are compromised. Kids with visual-motor (or eye hand coordination) problems also can struggle with writing. They have trouble putting on paper what they're visualizing when trying to write. In addition, for those who are dyslexic and struggle with reading, the writing process invariably lags far behind wherever the child is in his reading ability.

If you were to converse with Michael on a range of subjects, such as animals, dinosaurs, or the solar system, he could talk your ears off in lucid and interesting ways. He also told stories easily and coherently. This was a very verbal child, but none of this showed up in his scrunched-up and limited writing.

TAKEAWAY POINT

Open-ended writing can be problematic for struggling children. Writing is directly related to the skill of active working memory. If your child has been evaluated, check your child's active working memory factor on the WISC-IV. If the score is below average (say below the 30th percentile), chances are your child will be struggling with writing. You will need to help structure the writing process for your child. Find a good writing tutor who understands how to help structure writing differently.

TRY THIS

If your child is struggling with open-ended writing, often he has great difficulty getting started. Have your child map out a few stick figure pictures or other simple pictures that can help him with a few ideas before proceeding to write. This approach may get the child started and provide a bit more structure to the process.

Opposite Approach to Open-Ended Writing

For young Michael, mentioned above, writing was simply too difficult, and the teacher's approach caused him frustration and embarrassment. He was particularly embarrassed when the teacher posted the children's writing samples on the walls for visitors to see. Even at the age of seven and a half, Michael was acutely aware of how lacking his writing sample was, compared to the others on display.

Michael would like school much more if he could approach writing in more digestible bites. Then he wouldn't feel so overwhelmed.

Open-ended writing can be dreadfully difficult to school-struggling children. They find the task to be overwhelming on all levels. Typically, schools recommend occupational therapy (OT) to address the issue.

While OT is a valid approach to start with, it really addresses the lowest level of the process—the fine-motor/motor-planning aspects of writing.

To address writing difficulty, the "therapy" needed is long-term and laborious. As whole language is the opposite of the approaches needed for struggling readers (Orton-Gillingham methods), structured multisensory writing is the opposite of open-ended writing methods.

With structured approaches you start at the smallest possible sentence level, that is, two-word sentences. Children are trained to see that every sentence has at least a square (noun) and a triangle (verb).

Kids practice mastering two-word sentences. When they have this skill mastered, they move on to adding other elements to the sentence, such as an article (circle) and adjective (diamond):

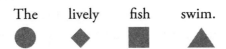

This method helps children to have visual anchors. The simple level of sentence structure is practiced in many different ways and with some variation. From there, more complex sentences can be introduced.

Once different sentence styles are mastered, the child can work on the concept of one paragraph, with a topic sentence and four or five supporting sentences.

This is a highly sequential, skill-mastery approach to writing development. It is contrary to the more popular open-ended approach that is the norm in schools across the country. It may not be quite as glitzy or as much fun, but it is an approach that our struggling 40 percent of the school population can get their minds around.

Practicing such simple sentences as "Dogs run" or "People walk," and building on them in a scaffold-like approach, gives children like Michael a sense of confidence.

TAKEAWAY POINT

Children who struggle with open-ended writing are in need of a different approach. Systematic, step-by-step skill development in writing is beneficial for such children. Such approaches take time, and require the commitment of a knowledgeable tutor. Landmark College's writing method and Diana Hanbury King's *Writing Skills* (Educators Publishing Service) also provide more information about this structured, step-by-step approach to writing development. Avoid more creative approaches to writing development (i.e., "write how you feel") until your child has mastered basic writing skills in the step-by-step approach.

TRY THIS

If your child is struggling with writing, seek help. You need to find someone who is comfortable with structured, direct instruction. Be sure to interview the tutor as to their approach. If they are not comfortable with more structured approaches to developing discrete writing skills, you should consider finding someone who is confident in this type of methodology. Systematic, direct, and structured approaches tend to work best for the struggling child.

An Old-Fashioned Child Advocate

I see my father in my mind's eye. He is about thirty; I am five or six. For his summer job he is director of a camp at the Edgewood

Inn, a hotel in the Catskill Mountains. I see Mel in a pool with about twenty kids. Everyone is having a great time. There is controlled chaos. Mel is wildly splashing one boy, who is having the time of his life splashing my father back. The boy's name is Marc. Marc is blind. This is an image and memory that always stayed with me.

Months afterward, my dad got a thank-you letter from Marc written in Braille. Marc's parents translated the letter and told Mel that before that summer, Marc never had the experience of being just like all the other kids. They owed it to Mel's instincts for including Marc, a blind boy who had never before horsed around with others in a pool.

My dad, Mel, or Mr. Selznick to those who knew him at school, was principal of PS 22, assistant principal of IS 27 and IS 69, and a teacher at PS 49. He was also influential to innumerable kids at the SIJCC (Staten Island Jewish Community Center). My dad was always fixated on human relations, having come up in an era where people actually discussed human relations in their coursework, in social agencies, and in education.

Harvey Araton, a kid from the Staten Island projects and later the author of numerous books and a columnist with the *New York Times*, wrote a tribute to the influence of Mel at the time of his passing away:

> He made me, a kid from the West Brighton projects with few connections to the Jewish community at large, feel like a part of a family. He never once asked me if my dues were fully paid, which, of course, they usually weren't. When I knew it, when I walked into the building just hoping I wouldn't be sent home, embarrassed in front of all these new kids in my life by whom I wanted desperately to be accepted, Mel would catch my eye and

mouth the words, "Go get dressed." The last thing this man would have done was to send a kid home.

He took me in and he took my friends from the projects in, too. Didn't matter to Mel if they were Jewish, white, black. They didn't have any more money to spend at the Center than I did, but they wanted to play, they wanted to belong. That was good enough for Mel, who taught us a few things about compassion and inclusion.

A generation ago, when parents didn't stand on the sidelines and scrutinize their children at play the way we do now, it was Mel who watched over us. He applauded our successes, consoled us when we failed. My father didn't know much about sports, but I will never forget the awards breakfast when Mel ticked off my achievements before calling me up to receive the Weissglass award (a JCC award). My father left the Center thinking his son was the Jewish Jim Thorpe. Poor guy. How was he to know that it was just Mel being Mel, the best advocate any of us ever had.

Long before 504 Plans, Special Ed Law, attorneys, medical doctors and psychologists, Mel understood inclusion and accommodations. He didn't need it all documented; it was embodied in his actions.

May you rest in peace, Mel.

TAKEAWAY POINT

There were instinctive things that my dad did to make sure that "outlying" children wouldn't feel so much on the outside. It doesn't take legal plans or IEPs to help children feel like they are valued and a part of things. It does take good instincts for children, though, and a willingness to go a bit against the tide of political correctness.

Struggling on the School Road (ADHD and Related Issues): Summary Points

1. When considering questions of ADHD, understand that there is an array of complex variables that need to be considered, especially the child's skill development with reading, spelling, and writing.

2. If you are seeking outside professional support, try to understand the professional's orientation before committing to any specific treatment. It is always better to go from a broadbased assessment that considers various domains (i.e., visual, auditory, fine-motor) before going to more specific domains. Once a specific area is identified, you will be in a better position to target an area for remediation.

3. Professionals will often see the problem from their professional vantage point or their own window; this may influence the recommendations.

4. Medication (stimulants) can be very helpful, but there will be large amounts of time where the medication is out of the child's system (evening) and not offering much benefit. Having an array of non-medical approaches and strategies as to how to approach and manage your child during those times is helpful. Also, while medication may help a child to focus better, do not expect skills (i.e., reading, spelling, writing) to be improved. The skills will need direct skill training.

5. 504 Plans can be helpful, but often they are unrealistic or they may not be specific enough to the child. Too often the plans are a boilerplate checklist of standard accommodations. It is probably better to use common sense and easily

manageable accommodations. Try to steer the school to use clear language in their 504 Plans or IEPs. Just checking off templated items on a checklist does not target the child's individualized needs. Put the goals in plain English!

6. Ask yourself what basic accommodations would be helpful to your child. Come up with three or four at the most, on average. Remember the notion is to help level the playing field for the person with the disability. These should be discussed in a meeting with appropriate school personnel.

7. Many children fall into a zone where they are not eligible for services, as they do not qualify as disabled. That does not mean they are fine and do not need any help. It may mean that you have to seek this help outside of school.

8. The overall IQ score is an average of indexes—it does not tell that much of the story. The child's profile of scores is much more revealing of good diagnostic information.

9. There is no "fixing" with a child. There is skill development and improvement. Target skills with sensible approaches that are supported in the research and in clinical practice and the skills should improve over time.

10. Open-ended writing can be particularly troubling for children. While occupational therapy services can be beneficial, understand that there is much more to becoming proficient in writing than receiving this level of service. Children need to learn how to write with direct instruction in a highly structured, one-step-at-a-time approach.

11. Inclusion classes provide support but usually not specialized, direct individualized instruction. While support helps keep the child afloat, it does not improve her skill weaknesses. Struggling children need explicit, direct instruction. No one likes to work at levels of frustration. Keep advocating if you find your child is in over her head.

PART THREE

Struggling on the Organizational Road

———————

By the time a child is in fourth grade, parents start to hear messages that the child has arrived in the big leagues. The babying and hand holding that took place in the early elementary grades will no longer predominate, say the teachers to anxious parents at the beginning of the upper elementary grades.

There are those kids who, by fourth grade, can steer their boat pretty effectively. They set their alarms, get out of bed, and have their backpacks ready to go. Homework is rarely an issue—it arrives fully completed and on time. Even at this age these kids understand the concept of time management and are able to plan accordingly. Projects and long-term assignments are handled independently. Such internalized life skills carry over to middle school and high school, serving the child well when she arrives in college. Without being sexist about it, and recognizing that I am generalizing, it is my impression that more girls are in this category of self-steering their boats than are boys.

Then there are the kids whose backpacks are like small trash compactors. Homework may land in their backpack, but it is crammed in with little sense that it may need to be retrieved the next day. Lockers are the same. If you go into one of their lockers after about two months or so, it is like an archaeological dig with layers of the past piling in on each other. Previous tests, homework assignments, notes that were to be sent home to parents, important and unimportant papers, and a host of other things compete for the small locker space.

In addition, these kids don't plan or manage their time. Procrastination runs deep. The pain of the present and the desire to avoid it far outweigh the perceived down-the-road pain of annoyed parents and bad grades. It is the present pain that is intolerable. Down the road is just that and the kids take a bet of some kind—"I will take this bet now and avoid what I have to do, as maybe I can beat the rap down the road and get out of it. Better than doing this stupid writing project," goes the thought process.

The children with these organizational, time management issues are turning their parents' hair grayer by the day. There is nothing like not handing in homework or not studying for a test (or not even knowing that a test is taking place) to activate parents' anxiety, and then their anger. It is my impression that about 80 percent of the yelling that takes place around school issues is tied into these problems.

The current view is to look at these children as having "executive function" disorders, meaning their frontal lobes are not fully matured. Many of the chapters that follow concern these problems of executive functioning and organizational difficulties.

Executive Function Deficits: Floppy Rudders

Every ten years or so in education and psychology there is a trendy hot topic or new term that was essentially unheard of the previous decade. *Executive function deficits* is one of those terms. Prior to 2000, very few people were making reference to executive functions, whereas now it is becoming commonplace. Parents will even state up front (before the child has even been tested) that they think their child has problems with executive functioning.

While I tend to not embrace too many educational trends, this conceptualization of where and why children struggle makes a lot of sense to me. I have heard enough discussion about executive functioning in conferences and interacted with scores of children and their families to know that it is a very real concept and one that needs increasing understanding.

When I work with parents, I do all I can to stay away from jargon, preferring to translate terms into metaphors and imagery that the parents can better understand.

Trying to explain executive function deficits to parents, I use the imagery that the boat is being steered by a very floppy rudder. (You could also imagine an orchestra without its leader.)

Take Brett, age fourteen, in ninth grade. Bright, creative, witty, charming, and personable, Brett is an absolute pleasure on so many levels. When it comes to managing his time and facing his "pain" (i.e., homework) on a day-to-day basis, though, Brett has given his parents fits for a number of years.

Kids like Brett are almost immune to becoming organized. Well-intended study-skills training, along with appeals to Brett's higher self, seem to miss the mark. It's like he wears a thick organizational skill raincoat that keeps such skills away from him, so these are never internalized.

If kids like Brett are so resistant to changing or acquiring theses skills, what is the answer?

Change can come in small, incremental steps when the person is mature enough to embrace his or her deficits and seek alternatives. In other words, these kids are on a different timetable than the typical child in middle or high school. Most high-school-age students that I know have little interest in facing their weaknesses with executive functioning. Sometimes people with these issues do not try to legitimately face them until well into adulthood, if at all.

I know as a parent you are saying, "Yes, but I want to try to help my 'Brett' now so he doesn't struggle. I'm not content waiting until he is an adult."

I understand that and there are some things you can do to try to change things for the better, but the issue of maturation is extremely important and needs to be respected. Keeping the dialogue open with your child so he doesn't shut you down altogether is a good first step.

TAKEAWAY POINT

Some kids are steering their boat very effectively. Many are not. For those in the latter category, much of the difficulty lies in their developmental immaturity and difficulty with executive functions. Many kids with executive function deficits may not reach frontal-lobe maturation until well into their twenties.

TRY THIS

Don't try to do too much if your child is struggling in this area. Practice one small skill at a time until this skill is more internalized and has become part of the child's repertoire. Understand that most of these kids are pretty resistant to the structure involved with working on these weaknesses. Think small. Try to get someone other than you to coach your child, as this coach will receive far less resistance than you as the parent.

We Keep Telling Him, "You've got to be organized. You've got to be organized!"

Fifth-grader Matthew is driving his family crazy. The nightly ritual of "What do you have for homework?…Did you hand in your work?…When are you going to get started on your homework?" is taking its toll on the family. Matthew's mother is particularly frazzled. With Matthew being the oldest of three children, this is putting a tremendous strain on her.

Handing in his homework and writing down his assignments are not the only problems Matthew has. Once he finally gets started, it takes him an incredibly long time to finish.

The other night, for example, it took Matthew four hours to complete his homework, which turned into an agonizing ordeal. Over the four hours, he dawdled and completed very little. There was much yelling back and forth. The temperature of the household was running very high!

Matthew's parents say they keep telling him, "You've got to get organized. You've got to get organized." That's like telling somebody with a bad leg, "You've got to run harder. You've got to run harder."

Matthew simply doesn't have it in him to "get organized." His psychological testing and history reveal that he has significant organizational deficits. Telling him over and over to "get organized" will not make it happen.

Are there any solutions? Putting the onus on Matthew by telling him "You've got to get organized" clearly is not the solution. Handholding Matthew more than you think you should will be necessary (see "The 10 Percent Solution" in Part Five). Providing Matthew with a certain degree of structure is something that must be considered. Without structure, Matthew will plummet like a stone.

The art of parental involvement, though, is tricky, and parents can clearly overdo it. Above all, parents need to not hold their child's age as a strict standard for what he "should be doing," as this will only result in great frustration (see "Age-Adjustment Strategy").

TAKEAWAY POINT

Being organized is a skill that many kids (and adults) struggle to acquire. Just telling a child to get organized will be of no value. Walking the child through steps as to what getting organized means helps to teach the skill so that it can be internalized and, over time, mastered.

TRY THIS

To help your child become better organized, start a ritual of going through your child's backpack together on a weekly basis (best on Sunday nights). Make sure every piece of paper is touched and reviewed quickly to decide where it needs to go. Let your child be the one to tell you whether it is a paper that can be tossed or one that should be saved. (See "Master Notebook" chapter for expanded discussion.) *Do not assume the child can or will do this on his own.* He will need the external support and structure of someone (the parent) helping, to a certain extent.

--- ---

Go Up To Your Room and Do Your Work: The Perils

How many households in America hear the nightly refrain, "Go up to your room and start your homework?"

Recognizing that each household is set up differently, it is hard to make generalizations about how and where a child should do his homework. The children of concern—those who are easily "lost in the woods"—have great difficulty functioning independently, even in a comfortable and functional workspace that has been set up for them.

With children who show these weaknesses, your constant challenge is to find the "just right" level of parental involvement. Once you recognize that these children need greater degrees of structuring, cuing, and guiding, you can see that having a child go off to his or her room to complete homework may be a mistake. Think of these kids as free-floating molecules with little to anchor them or to bring them back to the task. Without some level of structure, they have difficulty even getting started.

An alternative that provides some anchoring is getting the child in the habit of sitting within relatively close range of a parent, preferably at a dining room table, apart from other action going on in the house. Ideally, a parent can be sitting close by doing quiet work (e.g., reading, paying bills, etc.) Just the presence of an adult sitting quietly close by helps to settle things down for the "lost in the woods" kid.

Some children may resist this type of structure and insist on doing their work in their own room. Establishing this routine as early as possible (say age six or so) as the way that homework is done will pay dividends later. Many teenagers with whom I work are particularly free-floating in their rooms. They have a hard time getting started and seeing tasks through to their conclusion. If they knew what the rules of the game were earlier and understood that the household functioned in this way consistently, then there would be less resistance later.

It's never too late to change the routine, but the earlier you create the tone and routine for homework, the better.

TAKEAWAY POINT

While it may be tempting to send your child off to his or her room to do homework, understand that the room can represent a place where the child free-floats. Many children need more of an anchor to help keep them grounded, preferably an area around the dining room table.

TRY THIS

If it's early in the school year, it's a good time to establish new rules. With some child input, let them know how the evening is going to go. Set some parameters and guidelines. You don't have to be rigid about what is being established, but setting the tone and being clear will help a lot. Try to make these new rules a part of the routine of your lives, so that they come to be expected. Once they are established, it will be harder to resist them.

The School Keeps Saying "Stay out— they have to do it on their own"

By the upper elementary school grades, the message parents often get from the school is that their child needs to do schoolwork on his or her own without parental support. For many children (the smooth road kids who can work on their own), that's exactly what should be happening.

Such children write their assignments down, take out their assignment book at home, do what they have to do for the evening, plan for the amount of time it will take, and stay with the task without too much interruption. When finished, they put the assignment back in the book bag. These children hand in their work the next day without too much strife.

How nice!

Sometimes I feel like I could lead a parade of families whose children are the opposite of those just described. The children in my parade would have tremendous difficulty getting started on a task and sustaining effort. Telling these parents that the children are old enough and need to do the tasks on their own leads to considerable frustration.

Much of my professional time is spent trying to coach parents in understanding just how challenged their child is with regard to these issues. Too often, parents will default to the refrain, "She's just not trying hard enough."

The child's problems are seen entirely in motivational terms.

The point is not to view the child as overly disabled or handicapped. When it comes to the skills of initiating, organizing, and planning, the fact is that many kids start to show these skills pretty well by middle school, but many do not. For those who do not, the ritual battles that ensue on a nightly basis can be horrific.

When the child has great difficulty with a sports skill, such as hitting a baseball, the mentality should not be, "Well you're eleven, you should be able to hit a baseball." The appropriate mentality would be conveyed by a supportive and patient coach saying something like, "Hey, let's take our time. Let's break this down. Let's make this simpler for you. Let's practice this at an easier level, so that you can start to hit a baseball."

The same mentality should apply to children and their organizational deficits.

TAKEAWAY POINT

For children who become overwhelmed with all of the work they receive and who do not know how to proceed, calmly breaking tasks down into smaller, more digestible "bites" helps to settle them down so that they are not as resistant and shut down. Constant nagging is not productive. Letting your child do his work completely on his own will lead to frustration.

Homework: The Great Battleground

Homework is one of the great battlegrounds in most houses, but it doesn't have to be.

Rather than making homework such an emotionally laden battleground, adopting a matter-of-fact posture while setting some ground rules can work wonders for resistant children and those with organizational (getting started) problems.

Here's the basic message you would deliver, presuming the homework is within the child's level of ability:

I (your parent) am yelling about homework entirely too much. Rather than yell, we are going to try a new approach. I will be sitting close by to provide you with assistance if you get stuck, but that's it. I'm not going to yell or scream at you to get started. If you choose to do your homework, that's great. I will put a nice green check on the calendar. If you don't choose to do your work, I will write a little note to the teacher letting her know that you chose not to do your work. You can talk to Mrs. Smith about it. I will not get agitated, but it is up to you to deal with it.

This approach accomplishes a few things:

- As a parent your role changes from screaming meemie to a more objective, measured posture. Ranting mommy takes on a different role.
- With this approach, the responsibility is placed squarely where it belongs—on the child.
- The inherent message is that the child will have to deal with the consequences of his or her choices, and that it's fairly black and white how things turn out.
- The approach treats the child respectfully as someone who is free to make choices.

TAKEAWAY POINT

Homework can be a great battleground, a zone of tremendous conflict in the house. The more you adopt matter-of-fact postures and place the responsibility on the child, where it belongs, the sooner calm will be restored. Homework teaches certain values, such as meeting responsibilities, doing things you don't want to do, and facing consequences when you don't do them. The only caveat is that if the homework is truly over the child's head, then it is inappropriate. The homework should be in the zone where the child can handle about 80-90 percent of it without a lot of assistance.

Sluggish Cognitive Tempo

How many RPMs (revolutions per minute, as in a car engine) is your child's mental functioning? There is really no way of knowing exactly, but I have observed in children a phenomenon referred to as "sluggish cognitive tempo" that is enormously important to understand.

The children with sluggish cognitive tempos process information more slowly than others and complete tasks at rates that can make everyone lose patience. No amount of "hurry up" or prodding the child along will change the tempo. It is what it is.

Nowhere is this cognitive-tempo sluggishness more apparent than in their attempts to write, particularly with open-ended writing. The child chugs along while others around them are finishing the task just as they are possibly getting started.

What can you do if your child has a sluggish cognitive tempo? The next few pointers are things to keep in mind:

1. We tend to get irritated with these children. Try when you can to reduce your irritation by recognizing that the tempo is just what it is. It would be like yelling at someone with a heel spur to run a faster race.
2. Try to keep the dialogue open with your child without haranguing. For example, the following statement, when not said in nagging tones, may be seen as helpful: "Look, Benjamin, we know from testing you that whenever you write

it tends to take you more than double the amount of time to get things done. Even though the teacher said the assignment she gave should only take about an hour and half, that means it will take you three to four hours. That is just too much to do all at once. How about if we break it up into three small chunks this week? This will make it a lot easier than trying to do it all in one sitting."

3. You must try to explain the slow cognitive tempo to the teacher so the teacher doesn't simply see the problem as one of motivation or the child being distracted. Use real language—"His mind works at much slower rates in terms of his output than other kids, even though he is very bright." The point is not to offer excuses, but to state the facts.

4. With open-ended writing sometimes a jump-start can be very helpful. It's somewhat like orienting a person who is lost in the woods to cue them in to a direction (try this path) rather than letting them flounder along.

Children with sluggish cognitive tempos are largely misunderstood and frequently punished because of the way they interact with academic tasks, as well as in "real life." Sensitizing those who work with your child to the fact that he is not working slowly on purpose would be very supportive.

TAKEAWAY POINT

Many kids have slower internal clock speeds. They do output tasks, such as writing, very slowly; they cannot be rushed. Children with sluggish cognitive tempos should be supported. As long as they are not simply avoiding the task, or fooling around during the assignment, they should not feel punished because they did not complete the task within the same timeframe as other children.

TRY THIS

Time estimation is a good skill to develop. Perhaps you can make a game of it to develop the skill. Have your child predict how long a task will take. Have him acquire points if he can complete the task within five to ten minutes. Talk to your child about what variables may have contributed to the time being very different than what was predicted.

Weighing the Pain

As a child, which pain are you going to face? The pain of doing about two hours of tedious homework (that you don't do very well anyway) or the pain of your parents' upset when they find out, some weeks later, that you are missing your homework?

Kids with organizational issues tend to choose the latter. The pain is delayed. It's down the road. Maybe there will be some miracle intervention that will save them at the last minute. While the ADD issues are real, there is also good old-fashioned pain avoidance.

I ran this concept by Brett, the boy I referred to earlier. Brett was a long-term classic avoider and procrastinator. Various attempts to chisel away at these issues remained largely unsuccessful. In short, Brett was very resistant to facing his current pain. When I asked Brett about the idea of weighing the pain, this is what he said:

Yeah. I probably weigh the pain every day. I come home and know that I should start my work, but I get on the Internet and

Facebook, which is totally pleasurable, and a few hours go by very quickly. I do everything I can to keep avoiding the pain through the night. My parents think I'm up in my room doing my work, but really I'm just goofing around on my laptop. I spend hours on YouTube. I know that my parents will generally fall asleep by about 10, so that gives me a few more hours uninterrupted. I sort of kid myself that I am going to get my work done, but that is fifty-fifty at best. It takes a number of weeks really for my parents to find out or for the next report card to come out, so I figure I will deal with it then. So I weigh the pain, absolutely. Eight hours of pleasure vs. the total annoyance of schoolwork. It's a slam dunk.

I appreciate Brett's honesty. I have known him for some time and know that what he says is putting it pretty squarely on the line.

Most boys have this weighing-the-pain issue in spades; some girls do, too, but for some reason they seem better able to face it, in general.

This pain-avoidance thing is also part of the human condition.

So whenever you hear, "I'll do it later," or find out that your child has lots of holes in the "meeting responsibility" section of his report card or online grades, there probably has been a lot of "weighing the pain."

TAKEAWAY POINT

Human nature seeks to avoid pain, and much of school represents pain. Some kids are particularly adept at weighing the pain and deciding whether the current avoidance of pain outweighs the greater pain (of parental anger, failed grades, etc.) that waits down the road. Many choose avoidance, and this leads to much anguish down the road. Pain weighing is a very difficult force to overcome, usually requiring a fair degree of maturity.

TRY THIS

Be realistic. As has been suggested earlier, sometimes helping your child to break the larger task down into smaller bites can be helpful. He might not feel like there is such a mountain to overcome. For example, a boy that I worked with recently was bemoaning the fact that he had to read a book that was about 160 pages. "How about if we divide ten days into the reading of the book— sixteen pages a day and you're there." The boy lit up. The mountain seemed much more manageable to him.

Anger: "You can't make me"

What do these behaviors sound like to you?

- Not handing in homework consistently
- Avoiding responsibilities
- Procrastinating
- Not sustaining mental effort
- Underachieving (by everyone's estimation)

I bet you are thinking something like ADHD of the inattentive variety, or some form of executive function deficiency. I know when parents bring their kids in with these behaviors, that's what I am usually thinking.

Something that nags at me, though, is the question of anger and whether it may be contributing to some of the difficulty. Often the anger is a reaction to some of the ongoing punishments that have been received. It's not that the anger created the problems, but the anger is additive, taking emotional fuel out of the tank.

When children are not compliant, especially in meeting school expectations, parents frequently implement a series of punishments ("You're grounded…You're finished with video games for a month…You're off the team…") sprinkled with a heavy dose of yelling, ranting, and haranguing.

How does the kid react to this? Does he go to his room and think:

You know, my parents are right. I deserve to be grounded. I'll get all my work done, so I can go see my friends again.

I doubt it. Far more likely is the following thought process:

I can't stand my parents. Their stupid punishments won't work. I can't believe they're doing this. They think they are so smart. I'll show them. I'm not going to do the stupid work no matter what they do.

That position can be powerful.

Ask yourself, are your punishments reaching their desired goal?

Punishments tend to result in a great deal of resentment and don't usually help kids to become more motivated. Usually, the anger needs some type of release.

If you think your child may be in such an angry state, one approach that may work would be to take a few educated guesses:

- You think I'm being too hard on you, huh?
- I bet you you're real angry with me now, right?
- You think I'm over-controlling, right?

When there are no other distractions (especially other siblings around), try one or two of these. Perhaps in the car, when it's just you and your child, it would be a good time to give it a shot. You don't have to agree with what comes out, but listening can have powerful effects. Releasing some of the anger may lead to less of a desire to "stick it to you" and a perception that both of you are on the same team—not opposing ones.

TAKEAWAY POINT

Anger is a strong force that can undermine all of your efforts with your child. Find ways to show your child that you understand some of her feelings, and you may find that there is a greater energy for tackling some of the onerous tasks, like school work.

- -

Pain Avoiders in College

Pain avoidance certainly isn't limited to school-age children. Many college kids whom I know are rudderless ships, bobbing around at sea, avoiding pain at all costs. They gamble on pain and roll the dice. "Should I face the current pain of my school work, or put it off for a later date (or never)?" Many choose the latter.

The chickens come home to roost as colleges report grades for the past semester.

The results stun so many kids who had weighed the pain and decided to avoid the immediate pain of going to class or handing in work, only to receive the later pain of failing the class.

"I don't know how I could have failed," Aaron, reported to me. "I did my work."

Aaron thought he was meeting his basic responsibilities. The reality is that he probably handed in about 60 percent (at best) of the required work, and of that 60 percent most was probably in the C to D range. At no point in the semester did he attempt to meet with his professors to discuss what he could do to make things better.

The truth is that on a day-to-day basis Aaron kept avoiding pain. On average, Aaron put in maybe an hour or two (at best) of work each week, even though he was carrying a full course load. While avoiding pain daily, Aaron probably spent twelve hours or more a day on the Internet or playing video games.

Another young man that I know avoided going to class, choosing instead to go to the computer lab and hang out on Facebook and a range of other entertainment sites.

The Internet is a safe haven for these pain avoiders. Facebook can be quite the narcotic when there is all this painful stuff like schoolwork out there to deal with. The soothing blue tones on the Facebook page are much more pleasing than the harsh white page of a blank Word document staring at you.

504 Plans and various services are available on all campuses, but unless the kid makes an active decision to take responsibility for his or her own learning, the accommodations are virtually meaningless.

Having a floppy rudder makes college a very difficult place, indeed.

There are endless ways to stay in the shadows and avoid the pain.

TAKEAWAY POINT

Is your college-age child a pain avoider? If so, you may need to have a reality-check discussion. Your child will need to know the clear limits of what you will or will not support. A good values-clarification discussion where these issues are aired can be very helpful.

Putting Fuel in the
Shut-Down Learner Tank

During the middle part of the school year when the days are darker, the kids don't want to get out of bed, homework's becoming a misery, and as the weather gets colder, the household tension meter rises.

If you can, step back a little from all of the academic tensions and turn down the heat of the household. Your kids are probably feeling overwhelmed by the growing mountain of worksheets that they can barely handle. In short, they need support.

For many kids, school is an ongoing grind. The ever-present delayed gratification (do well in elementary school so you'll be ready for middle school which will get you in better shape for high school, so you can get into college, then professional school, and one day you'll get a good job) doesn't work so well for our shut-down learner heroes and heroines. They burn out much faster than the others, who accept the delayed-gratification formula.

During the more difficult part of the year, resolve to do something with your kids just for fun. Play a couple of UNO games or a game of Trouble (they don't take long!) or find some arts and crafts project to do with your child. Recently, I bought a world geography coloring book and found it to be good therapy (for myself). There are many such books on the market that are fun for adults and kids alike. Many kids like doing something as simple as coloring with you—even older kids, believe it or not.

If you have a spouse, get him (yes, I know I'm making an assumption here) off the computer and tell him to play a game with the kids, too. It doesn't have to be a big affair like Monopoly—a five-minute game works fine.

Kids need emotional fuel to tackle the drudgery they perceive about school. Emotional fuel is particularly essential for those kids who don't derive much gratification from their efforts. You don't have to do these fun activities every night, but finding the time to play some games or interact over non-electronic activities puts some emotional fuel back in their tank.

TAKEAWAY POINT

It takes a lot of emotional fuel to keep your head above water in school. Anger, resentment, and arguing are major drainers of this fuel. Look for ways to bring some fuel back into the tank if you sense that your child is starting to become drained.

Study Skills Coach: Readiness Is Everything

It is probably an understatement to say that our son was not the most organized or disciplined of students when he was in middle school. Like many boys, the art of staying on top of projects, keeping his papers organized, writing assignments down in a planner, and keeping a scheduler eluded him. There were many other things preoccupying his boy brain in seventh grade, like saving the world from annihilation on Xbox 360 Live, or playing in his Madden NFL League, those sorts of things.

Like many parents who are concerned about their child's organizational skills, we hired a study skills coach. The coach introduced

Daniel to a range of strategies to show him how to work "smarter, not harder."

I can remember overhearing the coach's work with Daniel. My wife and I agreed it was just what our son needed.

Sometime after the sessions were finished, I asked Daniel how it was going with the strategies that he was taught.

"Oh, I'm not using that stuff," he informed me.

Somewhat horrified over the money we had spent, and also horrified over the thought that he would persist in his disorganized ways, I asked meekly, "None of it?"

"No, not really."

"Why not?"

"Well, I just don't see the point. I'm doing fine without all of that."

Well, there you have it. What's the lesson learned? Is it that study-skills coaching has no place?

I don't think so. The message I took away was that readiness is everything. The seventh-grade boy brain may just not be ready for the discipline that comes from the skills imparted by a study-skills coach.

What may look good to the parents may not be what the child's maturation level is ready to receive at the time.

In our son's case, he was just too busy saving the world and taking his team to the Super Bowl to worry about mundane things like homework planners.

TAKEAWAY POINT

When you strip it down, much of study-skills training involves helping kids to be a bit more disciplined and better organized. In theory this is wonderful—probably a lot of us can benefit from those skills. But before investing a lot of money and time, make sure your child is ready for this type of work.

Organizing the Disorganized—
Skill of the Month

My dad used to have a joke about me when I was younger: "You'll never be kidnapped," he would say, "because there's always a trail behind you. You will always be found." I can attest with confidence that organizational skills have never been a strong trait of mine and that I would still be a challenge to kidnappers.

As with most traits, there are two major camps—those who have the trait to a greater or lesser degree, and those who do not.

The organized keep their rooms pretty neat, know where they put their things, and manage to keep their academic world tidy. The disorganized struggle with piles of paper and remain stymied as to where put it all, if they even consider it at all.

Those who are plagued by being on the disorganized side of the continuum look on in envy (and mystery) at those who seem to have this skill down—how much smoother life would be if we had this skill.

As with study-skills coaching, the training for acquiring these skills may be tough for kids if they are not ready to take it on.

An idea that you might try once your child is in middle school is the "skill of the month."

For example, maybe January will be "Developing the Skill of Using a Planner" month. So for this month, you talk to your child about the skill and show her how to carry out the skill. Each night (without nagging) you review how it went. Offer pointers as to how to improve the skill. Be sure to offer reinforcement ("I'm proud of you") for a job well done. On a calendar, keep track of all the times the skill was practiced with reasonable success. Keep it simple, using a plus (+) for doing the task, and a minus (-) when it wasn't done. Offer some type of incentive for a week of plusses.

At the end of the month, the hope is that the child will be farther along with internalizing the skill of the month.

I believe that if my own parents had directly shown and taught me how to organize things, I would have been better off. But, then again, I might have been a potential kidnap victim!

TAKEAWAY POINT

It's not easy at all to organize the disorganized. In fact, for those who tend to be disorganized, it is often a life-long struggle. Try to isolate one skill a month to identify, practice, and reinforce. Keep it simple. Don't badger. Be positive and reinforce when you see the child attempting the skill.

Master Notebook: Keeping the Disorganized on the Straight and Narrow

When my son was in seventh grade, a certain amount of avoidant struggling was taking place. After a frank discussion in which I wrongly accused him of self-sabotaging, my son looked at me and said, "I don't know what you're talking about." He then went on to tell me about losing all of his stuff. Looking in his book bag, I could see why he'd lost it. Think of a trash container outside of a 7-Eleven compressed into a book bag, and that's what his bag resembled.

Some kids are naturally well organized. They know where to put their stuff and keep on top of things, seemingly without much effort.

For the rest, and most often it's the boys, organization is a constant struggle.

The Master Notebook Strategy, popularized by Joan Sedita, is a great step toward shifting out of compactor-heap mode. I have used it successfully with a number of different kids.

Essentially, a large three-ring binder is the hub of the system. *The binder never goes to school.* The binder is for the storage of items from the book bag that are seen as necessary for a later date. At the start of each week (Sunday night is a good time), you are to go through all of the papers your child is carrying around and make decisions as to which can be thrown away and which need to be placed in the binder. In the initial stages, you will probably need to do this with your child, but as he progresses and can do it more independently, you can step back.

The master notebook will not cure all organization-skill problems, of course, but it is a good step and teaches the child a major life skill (see all the mail piling up on your counter that needs sorting?)

TAKEAWAY POINT

The master notebook provides a simple, straightforward approach to helping kids get organized and to have a method whereby they can keep track of papers, homework, etc. This strategy targets the skill of organizing in a tangible way. Start early and the habit will become ingrained. In the early stages, you will have to walk your child through the steps, until she is doing it on her own.

TRY THIS

Start a master notebook approach to managing your child's material. For more detail go to Joan Sedita's Keys to Literacy website (www.keystoliteracy.com). Be sure to find the section where the master notebook is discussed. Reward small progress with acknowledgement, and perhaps a marble that accumulates in a jar to document the child's progress. When the child has collected a certain number of marbles, go out for an ice-cream sundae.

A Compound-Interest Mentality

Change doesn't come easily for any of us. Think about how deeply ingrained our personalities, habits, and proclivities are. Fundamentally, we are who we are. Parents spend a lot of time trying to change children, and I find that their efforts are a bit too ambitious. A compound-interest mentality may help in this regard.

With compound interest, our finances grow in small increments. Interest is paid on top of interest paid—an improved product is improved in little steps.

Using this approach with children, especially when it comes to having the child take greater responsibility for his or her own learning, can be enormously helpful.

Let's say your child has great trouble putting papers away, keeping track of assignments, knowing where to find materials, clearing out book bags, cleaning out a locker, etc. In short, your child has moderate to severe problems with core organizational skills.

Trying to get your child to improve can be overwhelming (for the parent and the child), and often leads to frustration.

Having a compound-interest mentality is a slower process, but the hope is that smaller, incremental change can occur over time.

At the start of the year (or really at any point), come up with a handful of skills that you think would represent real improvement in your child. Some of these skills have already been mentioned in this section, such as the use of a master notebook. Others can be found in books that discuss organizational skills (study skills) and executive functioning, such as *Smart, but Scattered* or *Late, Lost and Unprepared*. Focus on one skill for a period of time until you think the skill has been internalized. As suggested earlier, you might try a skill of the month.

Once the skill has been internalized, that represents interest that has been paid. The next skill that is practiced will represent improvement on top of an already improved product.

The key to the compound-interest approach is having patience and recognizing small, incremental progress.

TAKEAWAY POINT

Change does not come easily. The more we embrace this truth, the more patient we will be with children. Targeting and isolating specific skills and practicing them to the point of mastery helps lead to small, incremental improvements over time. Compounding shows that improvements are on top of improvements.

TRY THIS

Try to write down very specific skills that you think would represent real improvement if your child was doing them consistently. There is almost no skill too small. Examples would be:

- Organizes book bag the night before
- Places book bag by the door
- Has a binder for papers that don't need to go to school
- Gets out of bed with only one reminder

Make a list of these skills and then put them in order of what you think can be accomplished first, from easiest to more difficult.

Think of each skill as a skill of the month (or week if possible). Set up a reinforcement chart. I like to give kids marbles for accomplishing goals. So, every time she organizes her book bag on her own, she gets a marble and it is acknowledged. Set up a schedule of cashing in marbles for small rewards or treats.

Parental Grade Monitoring on the Internet

Technology is rapidly changing many aspects of our lives. Over the last few years, parental monitoring of children's grades on the Internet has become increasingly popular, as most schools have some type of Internet platform to keep up to-the-minute on grades and completion of assignments and homework.

While keeping close tabs on your child has its benefits, there are downsides, too. I wonder if we are just a bit too close up and whether this is affecting the mental health of the household.

I have not yet had any fathers report to me about checking their child's progress online, but I am finding that many moms seem to be losing sleep over an assignment that hasn't been turned in (as they log on for perhaps the fourth time that day, late at night, while they should be sleeping).

You can picture the scene. It's 2am. Everyone in the house is asleep, but the mom has been tossing and turning. She gets up and logs onto the school website. *Oh, no, not another one,* the mom thinks to herself. *He's got another zero. What are we going to do? Maybe I need to go into the school this morning. He's so nonchalant about this and he tells me I should stop going on the eboard to check. He tells me he'll handle it, but he never does. I don't think I go on that much. I only went on three times today and I saw both of the zeros earlier and now there's a third. How can my husband sleep through all of this? I don't get it. Well, maybe I'll check the eboard first thing in the morning to see if anything's different.*

Like Facebook, eboard grade monitoring can take on a life of its own. If you find yourself checking daily, you may want to consider taking up a hobby that can occupy more of your time. Seeing your kid's stuff this closely rarely does anyone any good.

TAKEAWAY POINT

Tracking your child's progress on the Internet can be a good way of keeping track of things. However, this may be a source of agitation for you and your family. If you find yourself logging on daily (or even a few times a day), you may want to reduce the frequency of checking. More than once a week or even once every two weeks is probably sufficient.

Struggling on the Organizational Road: Summary Points

1. *Executive function deficits* (EFDs) is a relatively new term that refers to children and adults who have trouble with a number of things, chief among them being task initiation, time management, planning, and sustaining a mental effort.
2. The EFDs are extremely resistant to change. Trying to accomplish too much at once is a mistake. There are some good books that deal exclusively with this (see Appendix).
3. While the school is asking the child to be fairly independent and manage himself by upper elementary school, this is often unrealistic. Just because a child is in upper elementary

school doesn't mean that he is sufficiently mature, from a neuro-developmental perspective, to independently handle the range of tasks that involve planning and time managing. These skills often develop much later in a person's life than the expected timetables indicate.

4. Providing some structure and parameters can be helpful. Household rules or routines can really benefit the children of concern. However, you want to be careful not to make these too rigid. Particularly as the child grows older try as much as you can to enlist him in the process, so the rules are not viewed as a control issue.

5. Most people try to avoid pain. Kids, especially boys, are particularly pain avoidant and will be weighing when to deal with their pain. They will probably put off present pain for perceived future pain.

6. Establishing a quiet time early on in your family's rituals may help to establish a calm tone in the household; this may become more difficult to bring about later on when the kids are older.

7. Anger may be in the mix and be contributing to some of the avoidant tendencies. The more you are reacting, yelling and punishing, the more likely that your child's anger is a contributing factor to some of the work being avoided and not completed.

8. Keep checking your level of involvement. If you are in too deep, then human nature will take over in the child and let you—the parent—take over the task. If you are completely uninvolved, human nature will also take over with the likelihood that your child will not care at all.

9. Compound interest as a guiding principle reminds us that small incremental changes lead to larger improvement over

time. Keep thinking about which little steps can be incorporated into the child's daily functioning and become habits over time.

10. Strategies like the master notebook are good examples of steps that can be taken to change the odds of success over time. Think of these strategies as skills that need guided practice in order to develop. They will not develop independently. Once they are internalized, they become a part of the child's repertoire of skills.

PART FOUR

Struggling on the Social Skills Road

▬ ▬ ▬ ▬ ▬ ▬

Perhaps no area of a child's development causes greater concern to a parent than when their child does not fit in well with others. Most parents watch their child's social interactions closely from a very young age and form early impressions about whether the child fits in, can make friends, and is welcomed by others. The pain a parent feels when their child is not invited to birthday parties, or when their child is the one being talked about when she does go to the party, cuts deep.

In earlier eras, parents were probably not as concerned about these things. Socializing was most likely not even a thought in the parent's mind. Kids just went outside and played. There was very little adult steerage or observation about socializing. Kids argued ("He was out!" "No—he was safe."). Sometimes they fought physically or stormed off in anger, only to return the next day. There were no play dates. Rarely was play (socializing) prearranged.

I remember that, because that was how we "socialized" when I was younger. I think we went out to play every day and I do not ever remember an adult directing us, telling us to play nicely or to share. When we did come inside, I don't recall adults ever telling us to use our "quiet voices." We never had "time outs." Every day my friends and I probably got into some type of argument of the "you're out," "no I was safe," variety. I also remember getting into some physical altercations. Yet, even with arguing and the occasional actual fight, we were back out the next day for the next go around

Things are very different these days. If you argue with your friends, or heaven forbid get into a physical altercation, a diagnosis will soon be forthcoming with numerous visits to the professional in the community who specializes in these types of things.

Nowadays, parents are quite concerned about socializing. Play dates are arranged. Parents hover and assess their child's capacity to interact. Terms such as *self-regulating* and *impulsive play behavior* are used as the parents talk over coffee. There is much spoken and unspoken blaming when their child is not mixing easily with others.

Then there are all the organized youth sport situations with the parents constantly scrutinizing every interaction. Back in the day (log cabin era), we loved playing sports. I don't think my parents ever saw me play one touch football or stickball game in my life. Who would want them there anyway? Yet, my enthusiasm for playing these games never diminished.

In addition, modern social life involves a way of "socializing" that is totally foreign to a previous generation's version of interacting—through video games or "chatting" on line. Many kids that I know do not go outside over the course of a weekend and they may never literally see their friends, yet they feel that they are getting together with them through things like online gaming. What will this trend mean as far as our ability to socialize in more traditional ways? Will children lose the basic skills involved in social give and take? The answers to these questions remain to be seen as our relationship with technology evolves.

School is another place where the social demands are a constant. There is always a social hierarchy in place, no matter what we do. Little else equals school for the level of social intensity that takes place on a daily, even minute-to-minute, basis. Children are snickering, making fun, ridiculing, and laughing at others, often before the day has even started. The school bus, for example, can be a traumatizing social experience for many children.

Like much else with childhood, we have "clinicalized" the issues. A number of different clinical categories have been created to explain why children do not easily socialize. Some children, though, may have great difficulty socializing yet not warrant a diagnosis. As politically incorrect as it may be, there are those children who do not fit into a clinical category, yet there is something in their makeup that doesn't get the social "code."

From my observation of children over the years, I do think that the concept of social IQ is very real. Either you possess a decent, intuitive understanding as to how to get along with others to a greater or lesser degree, or you do not. That is not the end of the story, of course, and there are things that can be done to help fine-tune a child's social awareness, but it is a hard and often very painful road when one lacks a type of social intelligence. This social IQ occurs on a continuum or gradient. It is not like a broken bone—there or not there. An incredible array of factors can contribute to social-skill difficulties. Cognitive variability, which is typical of many children with learning disabilities, can contribute greatly to social difficulty.

We put a lot of expectation on the child to try to fit in better by doing something differently, but I wonder if these attempts to help the child fit in are misguided. I used to watch my father, both as a principal and as a leader of teen groups and sports programs, work with the kids that he saw as the underdogs. These kids could be sensed a mile away. They looked and acted differently. Few kids wanted to buddy up with them or share a room with them on trips. In short, these children were the ones to avoid at all costs. Yet my dad found ways to try to get them to fit in better. He had strong "underdog radar" at all times. How were they getting along? Were they alone? Did they have a buddy for the day trip? These were the kinds of questions he'd keep in mind. If the answer to these questions was negative, he would do what he could do to right the imbalance. He couldn't make these kids popular, but he could reduce their sense of isolation. There were no 504 plans guiding him. He had an intuitive understanding of children and their difficulty in reading signals within the social environment. In the chapters that follow I hope to elaborate on that theme.

"I don't want Greg at my birthday party"

When my son was five years old, we held a bowling birthday party. My wife and I were of the mind that no one in our son's class would be left out of the party. Not inviting certain children at the age of five (which is done, shockingly) would be unthinkable.

When we told Daniel who would be coming to his party, he got visibly upset about Greg, a boy he insisted he did not want at the party.

I couldn't elicit the reasons, so I fell to the old, worn, parental responses, "Now, Daniel, you can't be mean (assuming that was the reason he was so emphatic), and we have to invite everyone. You have to be nice."

What could the poor kid do? His parents weren't listening. Greg was coming.

Well, as it turns out, Greg was a handful and a half. Disregarding all adult directives and limits, Greg clearly was going to do things as this five-year-old thought they should be done. None of the other kids wanted to get near him, and his parents were little help, since they were in another area socializing while Greg was out of control.

I wanted to go to my son afterward and say, "Daniel, what good judgment you showed in not wanting Greg at your party." But, I held my tongue.

What struck me, though, was how clear it all was, even at the tender age of five. There were kids who got along well, and you wanted them at your party. Then there were the kids who were seen as aggressive and pushy; these were the kids that you didn't want. This intangible code is read very accurately by children. It's a code that's hard to shake.

TAKEAWAY POINT

If your child doesn't want to play with certain other children, try to understand the variables better before making adult assumptions. If your child is one who seems to be on the rejected side, see what you can do to monitor and temper behaviors. In the situation above, the parents socializing in a different room while their child was causing difficulty was probably not such a good idea. Remember, the social code forms very early.

No One to Play With

A book that stayed with me from my early days as a school psychologist at the Hill Top Preparatory School in the Philadelphia suburbs was *No One to Play With: The Social Side of Learning*

Disabilities by Betty Osman, which has been recently revised. Even though we have learned a lot about social performance of children since the mid-1980s when the book was published, everything that she said in the book is as relevant today as it was then.

Sadly, we often don't consider the emotional/personal side of social issues (that often accompany learning disabilities) enough, and too many kids in school have "no one to play with."

Left to their own resources, these children have trouble navigating the social waters around them. Back in the Hill Top days, the kids and the staff often had lunch together and casually socialized. The boundary between teacher and student blurred at times, but it was great fun and I think we (staff and students) learned a lot. For some of the kids with social problems, having a staff member they could "hang with" seemed to make a big difference in improving their social self-esteem.

I don't hear much about that type of thing going on in this era of outcome measurement and evidenced-based education. How do you measure the impact having lunch with a kid has on his social and emotional development?

You don't, really.

The impact is immeasurable.

TAKEAWAY POINT

Learning disabilities impact social functioning. These kids need to have someone on their side that they feel good about and who can convey a sense of energy and positive regard toward them. In this era of measurement and everything being outcome-based, what do you do with the affective side of school?

Sharks and Minnows

Out in the playground, in the lunchroom, and on the school bus—really every possible school situation—group dynamics are always at work. There will be those in the group who are more assertive (aggressive), and those who are not. There will be many in the middle zone. In fact, by sheer odds, most kids will be in the middle zone, not leaning one way or another. (It is important to remember, though, that each of these zones has gradations. So, for example, there is a top middle that overlaps with the upper group, and there is a lower middle overlapping with the weaker group.)

One law that applies to group dynamics is that the weaker kids will often be targets for the more aggressive ones. It's an immutable law.

Bullying is a very hot topic these days. There are lots of initiatives to "bully-proof" schools. I'm sure that some of them are effective, while others may sound good on paper and in theory, while not working that well in practice.

Harry, age nine, is like a minnow that has a tough time swimming among the sharks. He dreads the playground, lunchroom, and school bus.

If you could tune into Harry's head during the day, you might hear something like the following. Here he is going to the playground after lunch:

Ugh, I hate the playground. No one wants to play with me. I tried to play punch ball the other day, but no one wanted me on their team and then they just laughed at me when I missed. Ugh. There's that mean kid again. I hope he doesn't see me today. He put a boogey on my back the other day then he kind of shoved me on line yesterday and then laughed at me when my books fell. I went to my teacher later, but she said I shouldn't tattle and to just stay away from him. That doesn't work. I told my parents, too, but they didn't know what to do. They just said to ignore the kid. I tried that. It was him that wasn't ignoring me. Oh, no the teacher is blowing the whistle and I see that mean kid coming my way. I really hate recess.

If you were to go out to most school playgrounds, you would typically see one adult (often the little lady with the clipboard) overseeing the whole scene. The sharks and minnows dynamics will always be at work no matter how many anti-bullying programs are implemented. An important answer is increased adult involvement. Enough adults need to be supervising the playground and lunchroom to reduce the likelihood of children like Harry feeling isolated and potentially victimized.

The extra adults also provide a refuge for the Harry types to stay close to, as they often feel very insecure swimming in these waters where they are seen as weaker targets for the tougher ones to feed upon.

TAKEAWAY POINT

Group dynamics are always at work. In places like the playground they become more pronounced, because there is less structure. Children like Harry need to have greater adult support than they typically receive.

Sharks and Minnows (Continued)

There are no easy answers for the Harrys who are out there every day in the playground. Some of the common interventions are to place Harry in some type of social skills group or anxiety treatment program after school. While these may provide Harry with some improvement in his coping skills and perhaps in managing his anxiety, it's hard to see how they will reduce his playground issues.

In this situation, one of the answers that I see is for an intuitive and willing adult to step up to support the underdog. Such an adult would do two main things.

First, he would engage with Harry more actively and provide a safe zone where he could come by and stay within proximity of the adult. The adult's presence would greatly reduce any chance of the sharks swimming by.

Second, if the adult is aware of the shark child who is giving the weaker one a hard time, he must let that child know that behaviors such as ridiculing, mocking, or humiliating will not be tolerated on any level; these behaviors are against the rules. The shark child needs to hear something like, "You don't have to be friends with Harry, but you are not allowed to make fun of him or to give him a hard time. If it continues on any level there will be significant consequences."

Finally, the adult should keep an eye out for those children who fall into Harry's style. Perhaps he or she could gather a few such children and play a group game together off to the side. The Harry types do not easily make friends or know how to reach out, so forcing the issue would be helpful to them.

One of the biggest problems is that, on an average day in the recess yard, there simply aren't enough adults present. While it may go against the grain of teacher contracts, perhaps staff can agree to have two adults in the playground specifically to help with the minnows. The teachers would volunteer their time and rotate among other staff who share concerns about these kids. I remember being a younger teacher and enjoying being out in the playground with the kids. I would imagine there are plenty of young teachers who would feel the same way, especially if their presence had the effect of helping a boy like Harry navigate the rougher waters of the playground.

TAKEAWAY POINT

Children like Harry need support in places like the playground. Having intuitive and willing adults on hand to provide support to these kids helps to address the problem at the point where it occurs. The minnow needs protection and the sharks need to be handled.

School Bus Blues #1: Riding Shotgun

Nine-year-old Ashley was having a terrible time of it on the bus. For whatever reason, other kids always snickered at her when she got on the bus. Once she got on, she sensed that they were whispering things about her.

She was never sure what the snickers were about, but she usually heard things like "fat," "dorky," and "she's so gay, she still likes playing with Pretty Ponies." Sometimes papers were crumpled up and tossed at her, or an occasional spitball landed in her hair. The bus driver wasn't much help, nor was the bus aide. They never seemed to see any of these events, and all they did was yell, which the kids totally ignored.

When I spoke to Ashley about it, my sense was that she needed some kind of protection. But what kind?

I then got the image of the old stagecoach days and thought it might help if someone could ride "shotgun" with her, someone like one of the tougher or cooler kids on the bus. My theory was that if someone who was a tougher type sat next to her, no one would mess with Ashley. The ridiculing would diminish. In fact it might just go away altogether.

I asked my dad, who was a retired principal at the time, what he thought. I knew that the Ashley types were his specialty and I wanted to run my idea by him. He really loved helping the underdog kids, but he also was really good with the tough kids and understood how to get them on board. Whenever he had situations like this, he would make a wonderful marriage of the two extremely different kids. When I told him about Ashley, here's what he said:

> The principal can call in one of the tougher types on the bus (boy or girl) to ride shotgun, like you say. The principal could say something like this to the kid: "Look, I need a big favor from you." (Tougher kids love it when you appeal to them for help.) "Ashley's getting teased by a bunch of kids on the bus and they are making her life miserable. I wonder if you would be willing to sit next to her on the bus. I don't want you to get into any fights or even to say anything to them—I just want you to sit next to her. For your help, we'll work out a deal where you can get out of one of your classes once in a while for a free period. I think you'll feel really good helping Ashley out. What do you think?"

That's exactly the "shotgun strategy" that I was thinking about, and hearing this helped validate it for me, even if it was a bit unorthodox and perhaps a little politically incorrect.

After I spoke to the principal, who agreed to give the strategy a shot, he appealed to a pretty tough kid named Angela to ride shotgun. Angela loved the idea. There was no way that anyone would begin messing around with her; Angela took her job very seriously.

Snickers stopped. No more crumpled papers or spitballs flying toward Ashley.

Everyone was happy, all because a tougher kid agreed to sit next to one of those whom everyone was ridiculing.

Sometimes simple solutions can have great impact.

TAKEAWAY POINT

In this scenario with Ashley there was a clear power imbalance on the school bus. Sure, trying to bolster Ashley's ability to cope may have some value, along with putting all of the kids through some type of bully sensitivity training, but the shorter, simpler, and more effective strategy was to try to level out the imbalance. Simply putting Angela next to Ashley went a long way to eliminating the bus blues.

School Bus Blues #2: "Get out of bed, Pop"

William, age fifteen, was harassed daily on the school bus, with constant insults coming his way. A sensitive child, he struck me as "chum" for the kids who were more shark-like in style. They smelled droplets of blood coming from William. The daily feeding frenzy on the school bus was entertaining for them.

William's parents tried talking to him about the issue. They suggested the usual parental advice of ignoring the kids. (Can you imagine a defenseless whale calf ignoring the circling sharks?)

When I met with William, I asked him about his parents. "What are your parents doing in the morning while you get ready for school?"

"Well," he said, "My mom is helping my younger sister get ready for school and my dad's still sleeping."

"Still sleeping?" I almost screamed. "Are you kidding me? How far is your school from your house?"

"I don't know. It takes about fifteen minutes by car, but the bus ride is about forty minutes, after the driver gets done picking everyone up."

I was taken aback. Here was William—a clear target for aggressive, shark kids—going through daily nightmares and being terrorized on the bus while his dad slept. My theory was that no amount of therapy or work on William was going to change the dynamic on the bus. He needed support, not some type of coaching.

Here's what I said to the dad:

"William is being terrorized by other kids on the bus. You can go into the school and talk to the principal about it, but William is 100 percent against this. He feels that talking to the principal will make things far worse. Instead, here's the approach—very simple. You have to get out of bed and take him to school. There's no way that he should be subjected to this level of terror, and since you are available, this takes care of everything."

The dad understood that I was giving him a bit of a whack. He knew he should be taking action, and my words just confirmed it. His son was unequipped to handle the unstructured and unsupervised school bus. A simple strategy would save the teenager much grief.

Amazingly, William started to feel much less anxious each day. He even started to enjoy school much more. Unfortunately, in this day and age strategies like this seem to be in fairly short order. The likelihood is that a William type would be put on some type of anxiety medication and effectively be asked to tough it out. To me, this is very wrongheaded on so many levels, not the least of which is the message that there is a disorder that rides in William's head. The disorder, in truth, lay with the adults who were not taking effective action to help.

TAKEAWAY POINT

Sometimes the simple strategies are the most effective. One could make lots of arguments as to why there should be other ways to go here, but I was thrilled that William stopped getting bullied on the bus and started to feel a bit lighter in general. Also, this strategy helped bring him and his father closer—not a bad side effect.

Shyness—Perhaps

Young Abby is eleven years old. Whenever she is in social situations, she has a noticeable standoffish quality. She seems to clam up at parties with relatives, especially if they are loud and boisterous, as they usually are when her relatives get together.

I am frequently struck by the explanation of this behavior as shyness, which usually implies a choice or a personality style. More often than not, I find reasons other than shyness, as was the case with Abby.

Like many kids I described in *The Shut-Down Learner*, Abby's medium was the nonverbal. Excellent with drawings and putting things together, Abby was much weaker with tasks that required her to use verbal skills. When there was too much language to process, she struggled and when it came time for her to express herself, she had trouble finding the right words. These traits became clear once I assessed her. A very real imbalance was shown between Abby's verbal (15th percentile) and her nonverbal abilities (90th percentile).

From my point of view, the Abbys of the world may appear shy, but the reality is deeper than that. They simply can't keep up, and few around them understand that.

Abby's mom said it well. "The other kids lose patience with her. I see it when I am driving Abby and her friends places. She tries to explain something and it comes out a little confused, and the other kids don't quite understand her. They may even laugh a little. They're not really being mean, but they can't help it. Then Abby just clams up. She knows it's better that way—otherwise she'd feel too embarrassed. The school doesn't get it either. They will say things like, 'She needs to speak up in class more.' They don't get her at all."

Having assessed Abby, I totally understand the mom's perspective. Asking Abby to speak up more in class would be like asking someone who had a limp to run faster.

Can Abby gain confidence as she matures? Sure, but that often doesn't happen until well into adulthood, when people learn better skills for social interaction. Children are much more sensitive and prone to feeling socially exposed, and will avoid potential embarrassment at all costs.

So, the next time the relatives start pushing the Abbys to "Come on and speak with Uncle Joey and stop being so shy," try to set them straight. Do the same with the teacher who says, "She just needs to speak up more."

TAKEAWAY POINT

There are lots of theories about why kids act the way they do. These theories are usually accepted without much consideration of alternative explanations. Before you brand your child as shy, or some other label, think about other possibilities. While Abby may be shy, there are other overriding explanations to help understand her. Language-processing issues will always affect social skills.

Pokemon and Dolly Madison

Recently I gave a workshop called "Bullies, Victims, and Parents: A Complicated Brew." Never one to be shy about offering my opinions, I sometimes find myself going against current political correctness. When I presented my notion that we try to help the targeted children become more self-aware in their social interactions so that they don't play into the hands of the more aggressive types, some in the audience got upset with me. They felt that I was putting too much on the victims.

A couple of examples may illustrate.

Young Noah, age ten, is really into Pokemon cards. In fact, his interest is a near obsession.

After we discussed some of the trouble he was having with kids making fun of him, I said to Noah something like the following:

> Look, I think your Pokemon cards are great and you can come in and tell me about every one of them, but the fifth graders around you are probably going to make fun of you because they

think these cards are babyish. I'm not saying they are right, but that's the reality. You can also come in any time you want and I will be a very appreciative audience. But I'm telling you, if you bring these to school, you're going to get hammered.

Noah got the idea.

Then there was Brandon, expert extraordinaire on Presidents' wives. It certainly was impressive that he knew which gown Dolly Madison wore to the inaugural ball and that he even knew who Millard Fillmore was, no less President Fillmore's wife's name. Even so, I gave him the same talk as Noah's. Effectively, I coached him to choose his audience selectively when displaying his vast knowledge of presidents' wives.

When I told these stories to parents in the workshop, some were upset that I was "blaming the victim," and not valuing or honoring the child's uniqueness. Others noted that I was missing that these children were "on the spectrum."

Funny, I greatly value kids' unique qualities, but I also have my feelers out for when some of these qualities may be getting them into social hot water. (It's a tough shark pool out there.)

While they thought I was guilty of blaming the victims, I thought I was empowering these kids by helping them to read the social signals better.

TAKEAWAY POINT

There are some who will feel that these children's unique qualities will be stifled. Others may note that these kids have Asperger's Disorder, which is entirely possible. But even if they have a disorder, helping them to be more aware of which behavior will or will not receive negative attention in school would seem to be a good thing for them.

Avery: A Water Torture Personality Type

Avery, age ten, is a Water Torture personality type of kid. You know what I am referring to: it's nothing particularly overt, but he is drip, drip, dripping people to the point where they can't stand being with him.

Avery does extremely well in school and is very smart. There is little that he does overtly that anyone can identify as problematic, but he is water torturing everyone around him to death so that they react to his every small behavior. Avery then is shocked when the kids yell at him, "Stop it (whatever *it* is), Avery!"

Needless to say, Avery doesn't have many friends.

So how is he water torturing? Here are just a few examples that occur throughout his day:

- While kids are writing, Avery hums and makes clicking noises with his mouth. (After five or six clicks, the kids are ready to jump out the window.)
- Avery picks his nose far too often, sending kids into reactive fits when they catch him.
- Avery—a storehouse of information—will readily correct children when they give an answer. ("No, marsupials are not part of the rodent family.")
- Avery chews food with his mouth open, which sets off those around him. ("Avery, close your mouth when you chew— you're so noisy.")
- Whenever the teacher asks a question, Avery thrusts his hand up, shaking it back and forth to get the teacher's attention. He probably has his hand up a good sixty times a day.

In short, others find Avery to be annoying. There is no sugar coating it: he gets on peoples' nerves throughout the day, every day.

One can speculate whether Avery derives some type of pleasure from the attention. Indeed, Avery probably receives some type of negative response from his peers (and teacher) dozens of times a day on average—that's a lot of attention.

Certainly, ignoring Avery would be a strategy. Try telling that to the other ten-year-olds around Avery, though. It's too much to ask.

Many of you will say Avery has ADHD and needs to be on medication. Others may say "Avery is on the spectrum."

Perhaps. I really hadn't thought of Avery in those terms.

There are always Averys in our world. Learning to deal with such people and helping them to understand the social code is part of the deal.

Can we be more tolerant of Avery? Can Avery become a little more self-aware as he matures? These are fundamental questions of social interaction with children like Avery. I am still optimistic enough that the answer is yes on both accounts. It's just the nature of things. It's the social dynamic at work.

TAKEAWAY POINT

There will always be Averys in every class. A supportive and kind teacher can offer Avery feedback (not in front of others), and work out a plan with him to positively reinforce behaviors that are not off-putting to the others. This would have to be handled delicately, so that Avery would not be embarrassed in front of the class. Over time, the hope is that Avery becomes more self-aware and the other children more sensitive and patient toward him.

— —

Alex—A Socially Reticent Child

Alex is a boy that I met when he was about eight years of age. When he was tested he was found to have an extremely wide split between his functioning in the verbal domain of intelligence (scoring in the 99th percentile) and in the nonverbal (perceptual) domain (1st percentile). The social arena can be very challenging for kids with this type of discrepancy. They are typically referred to as NVLD – Nonverbal Learning Disabled.

Reading social signals, picking up on cues in the environment, and coping in situations that are more emotionally stressful are just a few of the many things that interfere with adequate social functioning. In short, many of the kids with this type of discrepancy tend to come across as out of synch.

This out-of-synch quality has, indeed, been the case with Alex. It has become a formidable challenge for his parents in trying to provide Alex with a somewhat normal social experience, both in and out of school.

Here are concerns raised by Alex's dad in emails to me:

> Being Alex is like living in a purgatory, wanting to be social but lacking in understanding of how to go about it. How do I protect my son? How do I ensure he gets social/emotional support? Does anyone in Alex's team really understand the crippling social effects caused by the way he's wired?

Similar emails could be written by thousands, if not millions, of parents whose children are struggling socially and having a tough time interacting with other kids.

The Alexes (or Alexas) are children in pain who need much greater understanding and support than we currently provide. They are the kids hiding in the shadows of the playgrounds or terrified to get on school buses.

TAKEAWAY POINT

There are Alexes in every playground and school bus in the America. They are in a purgatory. They want to be sociable, but truly do not have a clue how to go about it. The skills that come intuitively to others and many take for granted are not a part of their repertoire. We need to be patient, mindful, and supportive of these children.

How Can Parents Support the "Alexes" of the World?

In preparation for a number of workshops on social skills that I was presenting at a conference in 2009, I thought it would be helpful to get some feedback from Alex's dad, Alan, as to what was and was not working for Alex socially. Here's what Alan wrote:

> I wish I had some interventions with encouraging outcomes, but we're still trying to do what we can with fingers crossed for social outcomes. Every once in a while Alex may bump into someone in the neighborhood and do something with him, but most weekends the phone never rings for him.
>
> I've encouraged him to invite a new acquaintance from school over; he responds in anxiety that he won't know where we live.

I talked to his case manager and resource room teacher at the school and asked if there are any kids he's associating with. There are two kids he talks to, who are in a lunch group with him. I asked if they could encourage the friendship and suggest for the boys to call each other. I think the school is aware and has some empathy, but not sure they have the time or know how to really structure socialization for a child like Alex with his NVLD issues.

So my weekend ended with a frustrated, bored kid who wants to have contacts, but finds himself alone and not knowing what to do about it. There is nothing in his social repertoire that comes easily as it does to other children.

I wish I could give you some pearls of wisdom for your conference, as I am still experimenting myself with small steps. Two weeks ago, I can report, he finally went by himself to the concession stand at the Little League baseball field and got a slushy...."

Parents like Alex's dad, Alan, hurt deeply when their children can't socialize. But the good news is that there are some things they can do to support and help their socially reticent children become connected, as I shared below in my response to Alan:

Thanks for the update. These social situations are always very challenging. It is my overall sense that kids like Alex need a lot more support from adults in social situations (playground, lunchroom, etc.) than they usually receive. The simple fact is someone like Alex doesn't have the social-skill maturity at this phase in his life to handle the open-ended, emotionally charged nature of the playground. It's all too overwhelming, and for Alex, sorting it all out and responding in ways that others won't ridicule him for is far too challenging, given his level of current functioning.

In terms of some of the specifics in your email, I have a few questions or points:

- Have you asked Alex which kids outside of the "cool group" may want to come over to play at his house? As a general rule, I find kids always shoot too high in the social hierarchy. Everyone wants to be accepted by the cool kids, but this is a huge mistake. Kids who are seen as on the lower end of the social pecking order will never be accepted by the kids in the top of the middle range or in the top group (cool kids). There's just too big of a gap.

- Forget the label of "LD" for a second. Who are the kids in his world on the less social, possibly "nerdy" end of the continuum? You know what I mean. Which kids are closer to Alex in style? These are kids you should invite to play dates; they don't have friends either.

- How about the lunch table? Who are the kids he sits with? Do you know their names? What are they like? What's their story? My guess is that the kids Alex is having lunch with are not in the "fast crowd." Often the lunch table gives you some clue of social dynamics. I would try to target a few of these kids for play dates.

- As far as waiting for the phone to ring, forget about it. The phone won't ring. It's the reality of these situations. You have to do it (make the phone calls) for him. You need to reach out to the parents of the kids that I am suggesting, and give them a call. Explain that your child doesn't socialize easily, but that you know Alex likes their child. My guess is that the phone isn't ringing for their kid very much either, and they will probably appreciate the reach-out. If not, they aren't the right ones, anyway. Also, leaning on Alex to make a call himself is not realistic at this time; he doesn't have it in him. The phone can be a very awkward interaction point for kids like Alex, who are socially reluctant.

- Stay away from using the term NVLD with other parents when you talk to them, unless they raise the term about their own child. It could scare people off, as not that many in the "real world" know what it means.

For any parent of a "Alex" with not-yet-developed social skills, it's important to know that there are real steps you can take to support your child and help him to make social connections.

TAKEAWAY POINT

We hurt deeply when our children can't socialize. Recognize and understand that they don't have the skills that many take for granted, such as calling someone and inviting them over. You have to do these things for your child until the time comes when he can start to do more of them independently. For socially reticent children, it takes a long time to gain a modicum of confidence and skill. Encourage your children to reach out to children just a little above them in the social hierarchy.

Socializing in the Twenty-First Century

Eli's parents are concerned. They think their twelve-year-old child lacks social skills, as they rarely see kids coming to the house or calling on the telephone. Eli, himself, seems not to be concerned. He thinks he has lots of friends and plays with them all the time.

Eli's version of playing with his friends all the time and his parents' version are quite different. To his parents playing meant going outside with a group of kids and engaging in some type of physical activity. They expect Eli to play for hours on end.

Not so for Eli. When he gets home from school he can't wait to play with his friends. As soon as he gets in the door he grabs a snack and heads to a darkened basement. There's no one else there. Eli logs on to his Xbox Live account and starts his afternoon play. Some of the kids he plays with are kids he knows at school, some are total strangers he will meet online that day and never play with again. Eli will play for hours on end.

For Eli, it's the greatest thing having a ready-made social life. You don't have to go anywhere, you're in the comfort of your home, and there are snacks everywhere. When it's cold the heat is on, in the summer the air conditioning is on.

On the occasions that Eli does go outside to play when some kids in the neighborhood make a half-hearted attempt to play a street game, Eli typically gets bored in about fifteen minutes. A weak link in the outdoor chain, Eli retreats back to the house to the dismay of the few "old school" kids trying to muster up a stickball game or street hockey. "It's just so hot outside and you sweat so much," Eli thinks to himself. "Besides I am much more popular with my Xbox friends. I mean I just missed a pass and everyone kind of laughed. Who needs this?"

I don't know where it's all going, but for those of us who played outside on sunny days and inside on wet ones, we can't help but be disturbed by Eli's social life. When social life is a darkened room in a basement with no one there, we can't help but wonder what this will mean for Eli when he actually does have to interact with people.

TAKEAWAY POINT

Modern kids' version of social life is often fundamentally different than what many parents remember about their own childhood or what they wish for their child. This medium of online video gaming is strongly rooted in the culture. The face of play for children is extraordinarily different than it was in previous generations.

Those Little Interactions

A significant percentage of social interactions take place in reading nonverbal cues and signals. For all social interactions there are nonverbal and verbal interactions that make up social interchange.

What happens when we greatly reduce these opportunities to practice social interchanges?

When I was in high school, we would call our friends and often the parent would answer. There would be the common pleasantries and small talk, "Hi Richard. How are you? How are your parents? Please give them our regards. We hope to see you soon."

Well, having recently had two kids in high school for a combined total of eight years, I had those pleasantries with our kids' friends maybe two or three times. Why bother having to deal with the middle man (the parent) when your cell phone gets you right to the source?

Is it a loss that our kids don't have to practice those skills? I would think so.

I love having EZPass and feel quite smug watching others line up at tollbooths while I zip through, wondering what their problem is that they don't have one. Years ago when I was little, my family would go to visit relatives in central Pennsylvania. One thing that always struck me, even then, was how incredibly warm and friendly the toll takers were on the turnpike. "How are you, sir?" they would ask my father with a smile as we pulled up to the booth. "We hope you had a pleasant trip." My father would say something kindly back. I never forgot those interactions. They added to my model of what social politeness is and the value of little pleasantries.

Now our kids see us zipping through the tollbooths feeling superior because we have EZPass.

Recently I attended a week-long seminar on ADHD. The presenter, a renowned practitioner in the field, was commenting on the loss of social manners as a factor affecting all people in society. "I smile at a mom and her little child in line in Starbucks and they shoot me a look like I'm a child molester."

His comments struck me because I have had extremely similar feelings in superficial social interactions (supermarket, café, etc.). The sense of social invisibility is becoming increasingly pronounced. As we cut off channels to learn the basics of social manners and pleasantries, our children lack models. For those kids who don't have easy or natural social IQs, this is particularly concerning.

TAKEAWAY POINT

Modern living has altered many of our normal, everyday social interactions. Assuming these pleasantries (smiling, saying hello or good morning) matter, try to be aware of them, recognizing that your child may not have as many day-to-day examples to observe.

Little Remorse and Not Much Compassion

As part of a typical assessment battery that I conduct with young adults (sixteen years and older), they are asked to define certain words. One of the more curious trends that I've observed in recent years is the difficulty that these young adults have defining two words on the test: remorse and compassion.

Almost to a person, their definitions miss the mark. Understanding that remorse has some sort of negative tone, the definition given invariably leaves out the part about personal responsibility and the feeling of shame or regret. Definitions like, "Well, remorse is like feeling bad," are typical. (There is no mention of feeling bad about something you did).

For compassion, I frequently hear that compassion involves "love," leaving out that compassion involves empathy and an understanding of another's feelings.

For quite some time I've been thinking about this, but it was the story of a young man who committed suicide—seemingly the result of public humiliation—that prompted me to put these words to paper.

Are we becoming a society that cannot define or understand two fundamental words: remorse and compassion?

Judging by the way I hear young people grope around in their attempt to explain these words, I think the answer may be obvious. The inability to put oneself in another's shoes and feel compassion starts very young. So does the feeling of remorse.

Perhaps we should spend less time continually worrying about bolstering our children's self-esteem (everyone's preoccupation) or their SAT scores, and spend more time engendering the ability to feel remorse and compassion and to understand what these words mean.

Just a thought.

TAKEAWAY POINT

Are we losing our core human emotions by degrees? If so, is this loss linked to the time we spend on technology compared to time spent on legitimate human interaction? There may be a very subtle trend in this direction.

Life According to Martin

Martin is one of my favorite kids. Currently in college, he loves talking about social issues that have affected him. Even though Martin has struggled socially over the years, he believes that he has a pretty good handle on how it all works. I think he does, too, and I enjoy hearing about what he sees in the social arena.

Martin talks a lot about the various categories that exist in high school. For example, there are the typical "jock/cool kids" and then there are the specialty groups, such as those that cluster around things they're into, like Japanese manga comics. (If you don't know about manga comics, don't worry; I only learned about them through people like Martin. What I do know is that there is a group of kids who are into them passionately.)

Martin's advice is that if you are not a socially comfortable child (as he is not), it is imperative that you pay attention *only* to the social dynamic of the group that you associate with, and not concern yourself with the larger social hierarchy or other groups to which you don't belong anyway. In other words, Martin reminds us of the timeworn cliché "birds of a feather flock together." So for Martin, who is strongly part of the Japanese manga comic group, don't even think about trying to mix it up with the "jock-cool" types.

"The best way," Martin says, "is to not worry about the other groups, but focus on your own group. You have to ignore the other groups. They won't accept you. If you're in the manga group, go with them. Forget the cool jocks. Only worry about your place in your group. If you worry about your standing in every group you will feel very bad and 'loserish.' The loser group should never look to be found…or accepted."

Martin also talks about the leadership that exists in every group (or subgroup). He is attuned to the notion that the leader of the group is a key for the kids who are socially challenged. Even if the group is seen as geeky, it has a point person, or person with more leadership energy than others in the group. To feel better integrated into the group, try to associate more with the leader. Martin notes that this helped him to feel more accepted, even though the group he affiliated with was not a part of the mainstream.

I totally understood what Martin was saying, and felt that there was some inherent wisdom in his advice. Some time ago a girl I knew said this, "High school is like a caste system. Somehow you're in a group, but you have no idea how you got put into the group."

Martin is saying the same thing in different words. It may come across as socially fatalistic, but the fact is that it's hard to cross boundaries in social groups. Instead, try to solidify your standing in the group of which you are comfortably a part.

TAKEAWAY POINT

Social dynamics are very powerful and hard to fight. Martin offers some interesting advice having experienced many of these issues himself. His feeling is to focus on your own immediate group and not to worry about your status in groups where you will not fit easily. Sound advice, I believe.

- -

Social Skills—The Last Word

There are probably hundreds of factors that contribute to kids experiencing social difficulty.

By their nature, kids with social problems tend to be outliers. On one side of the continuum are those kids who are often ridiculed and made fun of (bullied), while on the other side are the more aggressive and bullying types of kids.

No matter what the mix of variables, understand that there is no one program, intervention, or pill that will "fix the problem." Social problems are modified over time with a combination of people offering patient feedback to a child and practicing of skills, along with good old-fashioned maturity taking hold. Sometimes we have to let the child experience the pain of his or her choices in order to make some type of progress. ("Gee, I'm sorry no one wants to play with you, but unless you learn to let others have their way, too, then they are not going to want to play with you.")

As stated earlier, there is probably no greater pain for a parent than to see your child not fit in. You, as a parent, can only assert so much influence, and if you try to insert yourself too much that will backfire, too.

Watch the cues. Initiate a lot of nighttime, just-before-bed talks, when the child is much more open and less defensive. Try to stay away from any heated discussion. If your child isn't being forthcoming, take some good educated guesses to give the issue some words ("I bet you're really mad at Jennifer for what happened today, right?").

Over time, with all of your support and understanding, you might start to see your child making better choices about how they react in social situations. It takes a long time, especially for the kids who struggle in this area, but I have seen so many children grow over time that I remain very optimistic about positive social growth.

You may also want to monitor how much screen time your child spends. While socializing through screens is certainly part of the modern era, "old school" play should be strongly encouraged for a variety of reasons. Learning to navigate social give and take may be one of the most fundamental skills one needs to learn, and the concern is that with over-involvement with technology these skills will greatly diminish.

Struggling on the Social Skills Road: Summary Points

1. In all groups, social dynamics are at work. There will be the stronger ones and those who are seen to be weaker, with most falling somewhere in between. Can we sensitize the stronger to not lord over the weaker? Absolutely. We can also help the weaker ones, those who become victimized, to be more aware of some of their behaviors so they are not easy targets.

2. Playgrounds and lunchrooms are places where sharks and minnows are swimming in the same waters. Increased adult presence would greatly help to calm these situations.

3. There are often small interventions that can help to settle down difficult social situations, such as those described in the school bus scenarios.

4. Don't assume that a child is shy when he shows social reticence. The "shyness" may actually be difficulty with language functions and effective communication, or many other factors that are not readily apparent.

5. You may need to give feedback to your child about not bringing to school certain interests that may be viewed by others as babyish or immature. While you want to value and support your child's uniqueness and specialness, understand that kids can be tough. You want to sensitize the child who is not on the more socially assertive side to better understand these issues.

6. Recognize that changes in the way that we interact in society due to technology reduce the opportunities for children to observe social pleasantries (such as speaking to the toll taker). Watch for opportunities to build in these interactions with your child.

7. A great deal of attention goes toward "bully prevention" these days. It is important to understand that the issues are often quite complex. If your child is being bullied, try to elicit from them what is taking place. Nighttime conversations before bed can increase the odds that your child will be forthcoming and tell you what is happening. Respect the child's wishes in terms of how the problem will be handled—it is important not to bypass their feelings on this subject.

8. The modern kids' version of socializing is very different from what many of us remember from our childhood. Playing

outside for hours on end with the neighborhood kids may be (sadly) a much less common activity today.

9. Even if a child has an identified disorder it does not mean that you can't offer them supportive and (often) direct feedback. This feedback can make a difference in sensitizing the child to social situations and their own involvement in them.

10. Watch out for parental overreaction or over-involvement. Probably the best thing you can do with children is to patiently listen and understand. If your solutions come across to the child as too rapid or going against the child's wishes, they will not trust you and will not be forthcoming in the future. As a guiding principle, listen a lot and react less.

PART FIVE

Struggling on the Parenting Road

———————

It has almost become a cliché that we are not given a manual when we have children. More and more, as life appears to add layers of complexity that are difficult to navigate, it seems that we need such a manual. Seemingly endless questions arise as to how to handle certain childhood issues and situations.

In earlier times it was more likely that multiple generations were available to offer their perspective, experience, and guidance. I know that when we raised our children, my wife and I were on our own. We didn't have the ready availability of older generations from whose acquired wisdom we could draw. There were many times when I sensed this loss.

In parents' interactions with children, communication can become quite frayed and strained, with a great deal of yelling and defensiveness occurring. When children are on the rockier road, the communication tends to be more tense and irritable. Parents feel frustrated by their child's struggling. Even parents who seem fairly balanced and understanding toward their struggling child are often pulled into interactions that are fraught with tension and yelling—mostly around school compliance issues.

Children with learning problems have a tough time managing the communication with their parents. (Really, many children have trouble with this—not just those with learning problems—but the struggling children are at a decided disadvantage.) Undermining the communication process is a variety of problems with language processing and language usage, along with perceptual deficits and other factors. There are breakdowns in the way the messages are sent and the way that they are received. Many children have difficulty understanding much that is said to them. They can be overwhelmed by verbiage and the complexities and nuances of the message. This creates an interaction that leaves much room for misunderstanding to take place.

Additionally, when the communication takes place in an emotional state, this leads to further breakdown. When people are yelling, there is no back and forth. If reactions have a defensive tone, there is no listening or understanding another's point of view.

Even well into their teens and college years, children have a great deal of difficulty conveying their point of view in a reasonably calm manner, or constructively listening to another point of view. Screen addiction is certainly not helping the communication process as far as learning in-person, interactive dialogue.

In many ways, so much of the difficulty that arises between parents and children can be stripped down to breakdowns in communication. If we can look at the way the messages are being sent and received (on both sides), much change can take place. With less emotionally driven communication, defensiveness will be reduced, leading to increased flexibility of style (on both sides). The change, though, has to start with you as the parent. Children have a limited repertoire. Parents are much more able to reflect and consider (e.g., "Gee, maybe I am too hard on him and coming on too strong. I will try a different approach"..."I wonder if she's feeling overwhelmed—maybe I will ask her before I start screaming about her not handing in her homework.")

The chapters that follow are largely about the communication process between parent and child.

My Head Is About to Explode!

Modern parents make you nostalgic for the good old days. You know, the days when kids went outside to play and basically didn't see their mother for a solid eight hours (except when she made them a nutritious bologna sandwich on white bread, which they wolfed down before running back out the door).

These days there's so much parental steering and interfering. Parents are self-conscious in the way they interact with their children. Just spend a few minutes in the mall or a supermarket and you'll hear:

- That's not your indoor voice, Hayden. (Ugh.)
- Remember not to run ahead, Connor, OK? (Oh, that's effective.)
- It's our special day. Mommy's so happy to be with you. (As the kid is disregarding the mother's statement while he charges ahead.)
- Now, Molly, you know you shouldn't use your whining voice. (Your whining voice??)
- Where are your listening ears, Emma? (Huh??)
- Or, as parents tell me how they're planning to get things done in the house, their language reveals how things will *actually* go:

- Don't you think it's time we started our homework? (No!!)
- Noah, isn't it time that we go to bed? (We??)
- It's time for us to brush our teeth, Ava. (What??)

Common parental statements like these convey a serious case of NBD (No Backbone Disorder) that appears to be running through modern parenting! When I hear these self-conscious words, I think my head will explode. I know that they will lead to kids completely disregarding the parent. In some ways the deck is stacked with the level of command or statement being sent; it's almost predetermined that the child will not comply.

Compliance between parent and child can be complicated with many variables affecting the outcome. Very often the sender of the message (the parent) is sending a weak, low-level command that is destined to be ignored. In our attempts to be nice and overly measured (worrying about the child's "self-esteem"), our message is not clear or direct.

Even children without complicating variables such as ADHD or language processing problems will ignore weak commands and act like they have processing deficits.

The issue is one of communication clarity and the manner and style in which the message is delivered. There should be a tone to the message that does not leave much room for negotiation or noncompliance.

TAKEAWAY POINT

Modern parenting is very nice and filled with theories on the best way to communicate with the child in the most psychologically soothing tones. Sometimes this leads to the child sensing that there is limited leadership in the family system, hence, No Backbone Disorder. Firming up the leadership and setting clearer directives will certainly trump most of the ineffective parent commands, especially those used above. Don't be afraid to be clear.

--- ---

Gumby Parenting

In the 1950s and into the early 1960s there was a great deal of stiff backboned (rigid) parenting, perhaps a function of so many men formerly being in the military. Children were often treated like little soldiers who had to march to parental commands.

If you haven't seen *The Great Santini*, it is worth a look to see Robert Duval play this style of parenting to a fault. A more modern example of this is Betty, the mom in *Madmen*. Soft and nurturing are not qualities that come to mind when you think of how Santini or Betty raised their children.

Fast-forward into the 2000s and we have parents who embrace Gumby parenting or NBD—No Backbone Disorder (see previous chapter). These parents seem fundamentally unable to call their children out on anything:

- Boorish and loud in a restaurant—"What's the problem?"
- Running wildly down supermarket aisles—"Why are you so uptight, they're just letting off steam."
- No social manners—"Hey that manners thing was so last century."

Like most things in life, the middle ground seems to be the ticket.

When there is Gumby parenting, no internalized rudder develops. The child has no steering mechanism and nothing guides his ship. This is not an easy way to live (for parent or child).

Start showing a backbone early (it's never too early), at those moments when it's needed, and leave Gumby in the toy chest.

Do not confuse this message, though with getting tough on children. Having a backbone simply means that as a parent you are not afraid to be a clear leader. If the captain of a ship is weak and indecisive (in action and in tone), trouble will follow. The deckhands will be fishing off the side of the boat. Similarly, if the captain is hysterical and raving, the deckhands will find ways to stick it to the captain.

Get clear with children. Lead with clarity and confidence.

TAKEAWAY POINT

Gumby parenting does not allow children to internalize their own steering mechanisms—nothing will be guiding their behavior. Don't go too rigid (Great Santini) or too soft (Gumby); find the middle ground.

Are You a Curling Parent?

Many of you who watched the 2010 Winter Olympics in Vancouver became captivated by the curious sport of curling, in which players slide a stone across a sheet of ice toward a target area. Probably the oddest-looking aspect of the sport are the sweepers, whose job it is to sweep ahead of the stone in order to reduce the friction on the ice and allow the stone to travel further and to stay straighter.

Danish psychologist Bent Hougaard coined the term *curling parent* to refer to those parents who insist on sweeping away everything that may get in the way of their child, their own "polished stone." Such parents are seen as excessive hoverers, continually making sure that nothing is interfering with or negatively affecting their child. They are always sweeping.

Another term that even colleges refer to with increased frequency is *lawnmower parents*. Like the curlers, the lawnmower parents look to smooth down and mow over all obstacles that could be in the young person's path. Such parents may attempt to call college professors about their child receiving an unsatisfactory grade. Lawnmower parents have even been reported to interfere with salary negotiations once their child becomes an adult.

Modern parenting has countered what it believes to be the sins of the previous generation's parenting style. But has the pendulum swung too far to the other side? Are we accommodating, modifying, smoothing, and making nice, to the child's detriment?

It would certainly seem that a bit of dusting oneself off (to borrow a dated term from another generation) and getting back in the game may be of great value to most kids as a life lesson.

TAKEAWAY POINT

Sometimes old wisdom applies. The wisdom of dusting oneself off and getting back in the game is often forgotten in the modern era of always wanting the "ice" to be smooth for our children. A little bit of friction is probably a good life lesson that may be lost if you are making things comfortable too often for the child.

The 10 Percent Solution: Is Your POID Set Too High?

Parents tend to be in pretty deep with their kids' schoolwork. However, by the time the child has reached middle school the typical message from teachers is, "It is time for you to bug out.

They are big boys and girls and should be doing the work on their own."

For many middle schoolers such wisdom is fine. Probably 60 percent or so of middle school children are able to manage their own school affairs without too much parental involvement. The remaining 40 percent—the ones who have trouble staying organized, getting started, and sustaining their mental effort—tend to need more parental input. The difficult part is knowing how much parental involvement is too much.

I find that when I suggest to parents in these situations that they should be 10 percent involved, as a general rule they get it.

What does 10 percent involvement mean in real terms?

It means that the child is largely responsible for managing his school affairs. The parent would help the child by orienting him to the task, cuing him in, and guiding so that he is on the right track and not floundering aimlessly.

The 10 percent solution means you turn down your Parent Over-Investment Dial (POID). Too often I see parents swirling around and worrying about the kid's homework, while the child has barely broken a sweat. If you're doing 60-70 percent or more of the worrying, why should the child worry? If I were a child in such a situation, I'd be thinking, "That's a good deal, keep going. Thanks, Mom, for doing the worrying for me."

It's human nature, no? Who wants to do homework anyway?

So, put your feet up, pour yourself a glass of wine, and turn down your POID to 10 percent.

Ahhhh. Doesn't that feel good?

TAKEAWAY POINT

Is your Parent Over-Investment Dial set too high? Are you doing too much for your child to the point where you're doing all of the sweating and, as a result, the child is taking it easy? If so, you may want to set your dial lower. While it may not apply to all children, and you certainly need to know the nature of your child and her issues, 10 percent involvement is a helpful guideline.

Hedonistic Pirates: Modern Indulgences

One day I was working in one of my favorite spots to focus down and get work done, a café called Jersey Java. Sitting close by was the unwitting subject of this discussion.

The café is a public place. There are lots of people sitting around doing what they do in cafés—chatting, reading, reflecting, that sort of thing. They probably were not coming to the café to be held hostage by the series of shenanigans being exhibited by a boy who was accompanied by his mother and grandmother.

Clearly this boy was the most special, most amazing living thing his family had ever seen, and he was being treated accordingly. Otherwise, what could possibly explain the fact that they never attempted to set a limit on or to correct his public behavior?

Since no limits were set, he kept ratcheting up his out-of-control behavioral repertoire. Stomping around the tables, calling out in a loud voice, sliding under and around the tables were all fair game. The rest of us, who were not as impressed with his "specialness," did our best to continue doing what we were doing. The mom and grandparents must have been very puzzled as to why we weren't clapping, cheering, and smiling at the boy's every move. They must have wondered how we missed the wonder of the Little Sun King.

Modern parenting is wrapped up in layers of theories about raising children, most of which strike me as pretty misguided.

Children, when treated as this boy in the café was, are in danger of becoming "hedonistic pirates," demanding pleasure at all costs. There is no end to their demands, and the parent (with this willing approach) is all too happy to indulge and provide a constant stream of pleasure.

From where I sat, being held hostage by this hedonistic pirate of the café, there was something very wrong with the picture.

TAKEAWAY POINT

Yes, children are special, but if they are so special that there are no legitimate limits being set on their behavior, they are at risk for seeking pleasure at all costs. This style will lead to others not wanting to play with the child and will impact their social development. (It's also not a fun way to live in the house.)

How Do You Measure, Measure a Year

Five hundred twenty-five thousand six hundred minutes
How do you measure, measure a year?
In daylights, in sunsets, in midnights
In cups of coffee
In inches, in miles, in laughter, in strife
                    —"Seasons of Love" from the play *Rent*

Here's another measurement to ponder. Research demonstrates that if you are a difficult child, you will be yelled at or reprimanded sixty-five times a day on average. Well, I'm not very good at math, but I do know this: the yelling adds up. If a child is reprimanded sixty-five times a day, that's 23,725 times in a year or 237,250 times over a ten-year period.

How's that for developing self-esteem?

In his book *1-2-3 Magic*, Thomas Phelan states, "The two biggest mistakes that parents and teachers make in dealing with children are: too much talking and too much emotion." The emotion he is referring to is anger.

Why do we yell so much? Is it working?

Perhaps there are other alternatives. Clear, direct, matter-of-fact communication can work wonders. Such communication can save a parent a great deal of wasted energy.

Take young Chloe, age nine. She's always dawdling when her parents need to get out the door; her behavior results in a great deal of yelling and screaming to get her moving in the right direction.

One day Chloe's mom decided to conserve her energy and not care so much. About half an hour before they needed to start getting ready, her mother said clearly, "Chloe, you can either get dressed and ready or we can miss the birthday party. I will be sorry if we miss the party, but it's up to you."

That's it. Words stated plainly and with little emotion.

Chloe's mother may have felt disappointment if things didn't work out, but whether Chloe got dressed on time or missed the party didn't matter. Either way was OK. No tension. No yelling. Eminent clarity of message.

There was no adding to the 23,725 ways of "measuring a year."

TAKEAWAY POINT

Difficult children get yelled at a great deal. They are children who tend to frustrate their parents. Yelling rarely works. A matter-of-fact communication style helps put the responsibility back on the child, where it belongs. Over time, this approach leads to increased learning. Self-esteem and household sanity will be restored and yelling reduced.

- -

Oppositional Children:
Rigid, Inflexible and Difficult

In many households there are temperamentally rigid and inflexible children who cause a great deal of distress. Possessing limited coping skills, these kids can become quite volatile and reactive to frustration if something does not go their way (hearing "no," for example).

John and Mary Ellen are the bleary eyed parents of three children. Their older two, ages eleven and nine, are pretty easy going. For example, when their parents ask them to get ready for bed, the children put up the usual fuss, but before long they are in bed, being read stories.

Essentially, the older two children go along with the program. Not young Ella.

Ella, age seven, almost always goes against the grain. If the family is going in one direction, she wants to go the opposite way. If the family chooses to go to McDonald's, she wants Burger King. If the family wants to play a board game, she wants to watch TV. When she is not given her way, or when she encounters even the slightest frustration, Ella wreaks havoc in the family. Intense meltdowns are an almost daily occurrence.

Two recent stories illustrate why her parents are so bleary eyed and how Ella challenges the household.

The other night while John was helping Ella with her homework, she insisted on writing a capital L in the middle of a word even if a capital letter was inappropriate, such as in the word *fiLm*. Of course, her father tried to correct her. Refusing the correction, Ella became extremely agitated, screaming and crying when her father insisted that she change the letter. It was a completely out-of-control scene that lasted about forty-five minutes.

In the second scenario, Ella went into a fit of rage when her routine was changed. She was used to being picked up after school and taken home. Once home, she counted on having a hot chocolate and watching *Sponge Bob*. This was her daily ritual.

But upon being picked up at school this particular afternoon, Ella's mother informed her that they couldn't go home right away because they had to go pick their dog up from the groomer. "BUT I'LL MISS *SPONGE BOB*," she screamed wildly.

When Ella was told by her mother that they had no choice but to get the dog, she became like a caged animal, ripping through the grocery bags in the back seat and throwing all the items around in a fit of uncontrollable anger. It took fifteen minutes before Ella even started to calm down.

One step in the right direction would be to try to not add gasoline to the fire. If your child has moved into a meltdown state, reacting emotionally to the meltdown will only lead to more intensification of the situation.

It is impossible to anticipate all situations (such as the dog groomer story above), but to the extent that you can let children know on the front end how things are going to go, the better. Two examples of talking to your child on the front end in subsequent situations like the above may help:

Situation #1: Ella, the last time I offered to help you with your homework, you had a meltdown when I tried to correct you. Would you like me to help you tonight? If so, then I will help only if you stay calm. If not, it's OK, but the homework will be completely on you for the night. I won't be angry, but I won't be helping.

Situation #2: Ella, I know that you expect that when I pick you up our routine is that we come straight home and you relax and you start watching your TV show. Sometimes, we can't do that. Like when we had to get the dog from the groomer. I am looking for you to handle it calmly. I will do my best to let you know ahead of time, but I can't always promise that I will be able to.

TAKEAWAY POINT

Some children naturally go against the grain. It is in their nature. Parents (especially moms) blame themselves, but you didn't create this. These children are enormously challenging. Reflect on this to try to give yourself a bit of a break. Also, the work of Dr. Ross Greene (see Appendix) is enormously helpful in understanding approaches with this type of child.

Parents! You're off the Hook (Sort Of)

Over the years so many parents have come to talk to me about children like Ella (mentioned above) who are holding their families hostage as a result of their behavior.

There are some who believe that these kids need a heavy handed approach. Nostalgic for the good old days, people will often say to me, "Don't you think they just need a good smacking?"

Well, many a parent has tried smacking a child when she goes into one of her wild, meltdown states. What does this accomplish?

Most parents do not resort to smacking anymore. They've evolved from the sins of previous generations. What do we do instead of smacking? Yelling and screaming are now the favored modes of parenting.

A first big step toward change (increasing the child's flexibility and reducing the number of meltdowns) is to embrace a few notions about these rigid, inflexible, and difficult children—the ones who go against the grain at all times:

1. These children are temperamentally wired for poor coping. Parenting is often not to blame. You did not create this situation. If parenting had been responsible, then Ella's siblings would also be melting down. These siblings do not show this behavior; they are flexible and easy going.
2. The inflexible kids have a fundamental skill deficit in their characteristic style of problem solving. It is this lack of skill that results in their rigid style of responding.
3. No amount of yelling, screaming, or smacking will help. In fact, these approaches will make matters worse.

Once you embrace these notions, then things can change! Guess where the change point is going to be focused? One hint: It's not on the child, at least not initially.

Even though I firmly believe that you did not create the situation, it's the adults who can reflect on how they are managing these challenging issues and then make changes by responding differently.

So, parents, you are off the hook (sort of). Stop blaming yourselves and start looking to how you can change your way of dealing with the child!

TAKEAWAY POINT

Moms will blame themselves and take entirely too much of the heat for difficult children. Difficult kids are difficult because of their temperaments, which have been present essentially from birth. Parenting did not create your child's temperament, but the focus is on parents to manage these children.

— —

"Thanks for yelling, Mom! I see the light!"

It would be interesting if we could take a psychological temperature reading across the country while homework is being conducted, typically from four in the afternoon to about nine o'clock at night. My sense is that, in many households, the temperature would rise steadily with every passing hour of homework frustration. If we could peek into these households, we would probably see increased tensions with a great deal of irritability and yelling.

In the run-up to every new school year, I can feel parents anticipating homework anguish.

Kids (and most adults) avoid doing what they don't enjoy doing. Their avoidance and procrastination results in tremendous family frustration. Emotional reactivity (yelling) becomes the norm.

When was the last time that you felt your yelling reached its desired goal? When did the child say, "Well, Mom, thanks for yelling. I really appreciate it and I will start to do my homework."

I think I know the answer. Yelling rarely reaches its desired goal.

But this begs the question, what will then?

This is a challenging and complex topic that does not lend itself to simple answers. Remember, you set the tone. Assume that if you lead in a calm but firm way, the child will follow your lead. This may not happen immediately, but if you set the tone and parameters, your children will come to understand over time what is expected, and will follow your direction much more readily.

Here's an example of a clear directive given calmly but firmly by a mother to her ten-year-old son who had a history of dawdling, crying, and doing anything to avoid starting and completing his homework:

> This is how homework is going to work tonight. I am setting this countdown clock for an hour and a half. When it goes off, I will assume your homework is done. If it is finished, everyone will be happy and you will have earned TV/computer/video playtime. If it isn't, then I will write a note to the teacher explaining you chose not to do your homework. If it is not finished then you haven't earned the TV or computer time. You'll let me know if you need my help.

This mom did not get overly invested in the result. She did not make homework her concern, but made it her child's concern. To some of you this may sound cold, a bit too cut-and-dried. But by stating expectations clearly, in fairly objective black-and-white tones, the mom gave the child a choice one way or another.

The key is not to get upset if things don't go the way you had hoped. Ultimately, the homework is the child's problem, even if you are available for support or help when needed.

Turn down the heat, but be clear in your goal and stated expectations. Let's try to get the temperature in America to fall within the normal zone during homework.

TAKEAWAY POINT

You set the tone. Establish your tone with clarity of mind according to where you want things to go. The dog wags the tail, not the other way around.

New School Year's Resolution:
Stay Calm and End the Shenanigans

It's that time again. That little knot in your stomach is forming with the start of the new school year and you are reading various articles on the top tips for your kid having a great year.

Here's my number one tip—resolve to stay calm.

School problems result in a great deal of tension, anxiety, and all-around teeth gnashing. Most of it is unproductive. As an alternative to the yelling and all of the reactive stress with your child, practice a different style of talking that puts responsibility where it belongs—on your child. This style involves speaking in matter-of-fact tones. Effectively, your approach would be more objective and less reactive.

Take a child that I saw recently, moody Meghan, age fifteen. Last year, Meghan's parents spent a lot of time and money taking Meghan to tutoring, much to her dismay. Meghan wasn't happy about the tutoring, primarily because it interfered with her all-important Facebook time. Each week, right on cue when it was time to get ready for tutoring, Meghan gave her parents an extremely hard time about going. In response, her parents engaged in yelling and screaming matches, trying to get the recalcitrant Meghan to comply. It was not a pretty picture. This scene occurred twice a week over the course of the previous year.

When the beleaguered parents talked to me about it, I suggested to them that they adopt an either-or posture with Meghan. Rather than go through all the hoops to get Meghan to comply, they were coached to say something like the following:

Meghan, we know school has been hard. We have tried to get you help. However, you resisted the tutor and gave us grief about going. We then started yelling and screaming at you. It made the household miserable. This is going to stop. We are not going to yell about it anymore. It's going to be one way or the other. Either you approach tutoring with a reasonable attitude, or you are on your own with your schoolwork. You decide. Either way is OK.

So, this year, resolve to end the shenanigans. Stop the yelling, and calmly put responsibility where it belongs.

TAKEAWAY POINT

Trying to stay calm when kids go into emotional upheaval is very hard. Set this style as a goal. Much of what goes on in households with children can be treated in more black-and-white tones. A key is to not be invested in the outcome. In the situation above, the parents need to be OK with Meghan's decision, either way.

What Are the Triggers?

Something I hear a lot from parents and teachers of temperamentally challenging children is the notion that the child had a fit or meltdown "for no reason."

It is my experience that "for no reason" is never the case. There is always a reason.

More often than not these reasons are fairly repetitive themes in the child's life. By understanding these reasons or triggers, we are in a better position to do something about them.

A couple of examples may help to illustrate.

Some years ago I observed a boy named Malik, who was prone to wild, explosive tantrums, in a preschool classroom. Malik's teacher did not see the triggers. She thought the tantrums occurred for no reason.

As I was watching, the first situation unfolded shortly after Malik had been playing with cars and trucks quietly by himself in the middle of the class; he had been doing this while the other children were in circle time. After the circle, the children were told to get ready for snacks and to go wash up. Innocently, a couple of children walked into the space where Malik had been playing. One of the boys started to move one of Malik's trucks, resulting in Malik screaming wildly and grabbing the toy back from the boy. In short, Malik went into an out-of-control fit when children came into his area. Malik's reactions totally shocked the boy and caught the teacher, who was off to the side helping another child, completely off guard.

In the second situation, the teacher was sitting at Malik's table during lunch. The children in this preschool were served lunch family style, with plates being passed around. Malik insisted he wanted two portions immediately. The teacher firmly held to the established rule of, "You have to start with one and then ask for seconds." This limit setting sent Malik into a crazed, ballistic fit.

Helping the teacher to see Malik's tendencies would let her identify the triggers so that interventions could be implemented to reduce the frequency of the child's meltdowns. Once the teacher moved away from thinking that Malik's reactions were out of the blue and for no reason, she would be better able to make better up-front predictions and reduce the probability of their occurrence.

TAKEAWAY POINT

Since we can't track and monitor all interactions that take place with a child, it is easy to think that the reactive fits occur out of the blue or for no reason. Try to get a handle on the triggers. These triggers repeat (even if the actual content or situations change). Once you know the triggers better, you can implement more effective interventions.

Dealing with the Triggers

A common theme among temperamentally challenging children is that their coping style results in out-of-the-blue tantrums or fits. Since they lack an adequate internalized voice that helps them temper their reactions (e.g., "It's OK to wait until the first portion of food is given out to ask for seconds), the child melts down.

When meltdowns occur, there is no reasoning, coping, or problem solving.

During the times when these children exhibit such behaviors, it is helpful for the adults to anticipate; the goal is to predict the likelihood of the fit occurring and to try to intervene to dramatically reduce the chance of it happening. Often, very simple and cost-effective strategies work without resorting to calling in the specialists. On-your-toes parenting is needed with children of this temperament style, who have lower-level coping and problem-solving skills than the more flexible children, who do not require such a style of parenting.

Returning to Malik and the circle time story, the simple approach we implemented involved having the classroom assistant stand very close to Malik during the transitions (e.g., circle time to washing up) in order to act like an air traffic controller and direct any children encroaching on Malik's space to move along.

This strategy was implemented once the trigger (e.g., Malik having difficulty with children coming into his area on a transition) was identified.

In the second story, with Malik wanting two portions before having the first, the strategy was to briefly talk to Malik off to the side just before the food was to be passed around. Even if the children had been told about the rule on previous days, for someone like Malik replanting this notion in his frontal lobe and anticipating his likely reactions had very good effects. Malik was better able to tolerate the frustration of not having the food exactly the way he wanted it.

Some people may object since such a strategy did not teach Malik how to cope better. My argument would be that these strategies were appropriate to Malik's level of emotional maturation. Given his range of learning issues and his verbal/language deficiencies, he wasn't ready for direct coping mechanisms. It was up to the adults to change their style of interacting with him to anticipate his reactions.

TAKEAWAY POINT

Knowing the triggers and the child's typical style of coping helps you, as a teacher or a parent, make adjustments accordingly. You can predict better whether the child is likely to be set off. Going forward from our two Malik stories, the teachers had very few meltdowns in similar situations once they implemented their simple strategies.

Cool Anger: Put Yourself in Timeout

There is one very popular parenting tool that 99 percent of modern parents use 99 percent of the time to deal with situations, and it doesn't work (99 percent of the time). Yet, we persist in doing it. This number one parenting tool is yelling.

Telling ourselves that yelling is effective, it becomes the fall back, default parenting strategy. And we bundle the yelling with, "Go to time out." This strategy also has limited effectiveness, as it is the rare child who goes to his room thinking about the error of his ways.

As parents (and as people) we think that when we are mad, we must reactively display this as hot anger.

A much more effective approach with children is the use of cool anger. Cool anger is probably more honest and impactful, but it is something that most parents have become afraid of using, thinking this will inflict too much shame and guilt on the child.

For example, let's say Gavin, age nine, gets into trouble at school by spitting at someone while they are waiting in line. When it is time to pick Gavin up at the end of the day, the teacher meets you outside. She is very upset about what happened.

A common parental reaction would be to yell at the child in the car and, once home, send him up to his room for an indefinite time out.

An alternative would be to make things very chilly and uncomfortable for the child. In the car, nothing needs to be said. There would be no fun songs or the usual "how was your day" conversation. Once inside the house, you would say directly, "I am very angry with you for spitting at someone in school. I will not speak to you until I am ready and less angry. Until I am less angry, there is to be no television, computer, or video games." Once that is stated, that's it—turn on your heels and go about your business. No yelling, haranguing, or screaming.

The approach is very efficient and sends a powerful message. Instead of turning up the heat and administering reactive punishments, this approach allows you to put responsibility squarely where it belongs—on the child. The hope with this approach is that the child will brood a bit, thinking about what he has done, and feel some remorse.

When hot anger is applied, less remorse is felt and the child is likely to go into a defensive posture (e.g., "You're unfair. It wasn't my fault. The teacher is mean.")

With the cool anger approach it is virtually impossible for the child to respond defensively and argue back.

TAKEAWAY POINT

Cool anger is almost impossible to argue with or to defend. When applied, it allows a child to feel a degree of remorse or regret for his actions. Consequences are not administered emotionally or reactively, but are a natural result of the situation. In the scenario above, it would have been unnatural if the parent had been nice to the child back at home after the child had done something like spitting. With the direct, cool anger approach, none of the usual add-on anger or yelling is necessary to make the point and get the child to feel a sense of regret.

What Are the Odds?

Las Vegas is extraordinarily accurate in figuring out the odds of a given event. Building upon past behavior, the casinos are very good at determining the likelihood of something occurring.

When parents come in to discuss their child's behavioral challenges, I find they are mostly reactive rather than proactive. They are not applying "Las Vegas odds" thinking.

Reactive parenting is just what it implies. When a negative behavior occurs, the parent reacts (yells), usually emotionally. There is little consideration of front-end strategy or proactive thinking.

Proactive thinking requires that the odds of a given event (behavior) occurring are fully considered.

- Did the child run ahead in Target the last time you went shopping (remember Ella's story)?
- Did she have a fit in the supermarket when she couldn't have exactly what she wanted?
- Was there screaming and fighting in the back seat the last time you went somewhere?
- Did you have to scream like a banshee when your child dawdled, not getting dressed, the last time you needed the child to cooperate?

If the answer to these types of questions is yes, then the odds of these types of behaviors occurring in similar situations in the future are very great.

If you understand simple odds, you can put a strategy into place that shifts the odds in your favor. For example, the child who runs ahead in Target can be told on the front end in very calm and direct terms, "The last time we went to Target, you broke the rules and ran ahead. This made Mommy very unhappy. It will not happen that way today. If you run ahead, we stop and go straight home. No McDonald's afterward—nothing. Even if we have to put everything in our cart aside, that's fine. That's how it is going to work."

If the child runs ahead, give a simple warning, and if this is ignored, then go straight home. Don't make a scene. No yelling, no screaming, no time out. Apply a little chilly anger and don't be so "nicey nice."

The next time you plan to go to Target, ask the child what the rule is and what will happen if she breaks the rule.

Seems to me the odds have shifted in your favor. That's a bet that I would take.

TAKEAWAY POINT

Front-end thinking (considering likely odds of a given event or behavior occurring) helps you to anticipate and put strategies in place before the behavior occurs. This does not mean the approach will eliminate the negative behavior altogether, just greatly reduce its likelihood of occurring. Over time, the hope is that the child will learn to anticipate better on his own, which is the ultimate goal.

Struggling on the Parenting Road: Summary Points

1. How do you deliver your commands to your kids? If you deliver a weak command, the odds of compliance are very poor. This is not to say that you should bark orders at your child, but check the message and how it is being delivered. Question commands ("Isn't it time we went to bed?") or

weak sounding commands ("Let's go to bed now") are pre-destined to be ignored.

2. School-struggling children often have processing problems and difficulty with language functions. While all children will struggle with weak commands, children with these difficulties need even greater clarity of communication for them to understand and comply.

3. Gumby parenting can lead to many child-behavior problems. Having a clear and firm parenting style is usually most effective. Watch out for being too soft, but also make sure you don't become overly rigid.

4. Do you believe that things should always be smooth and easy for your child? Do you try—at all costs—to not let your child feel any pain? Some of the pain that comes from a child choosing wrongly can be enormously instructive so that similar choices are not repeated. Curling parents do not allow such learning to take place.

5. Parents can be overinvested in all facets of a child's life, especially homework and school work. Turning down your overinvestment dial and being somewhat involved (say 10 percent)—but not too involved—helps create the right balance and puts responsibility where it belongs: on the child.

6. Children are natural pleasure seekers. Are your children becoming hedonistic pirates? Are you being held hostage by their incessant demands? This is a hard way to live, as the household can feel very chaotic when children exercise too much control. Again, developing clearer tones of leadership reaps enormous benefits. You may want to seek professional support in developing your clear voice further.

7. Yelling is perhaps the number-one parenting strategy being used to try to get kids to behave and comply. The problem

is that yelling rarely works. Yelling is reactive. You'll have much greater odds of success with more matter-of-fact tones that place responsibility on the child.

8. Child temperament is an enormously important variable that may not be discussed enough in professional circles. Children tend to fall into one of two camps: more flexible by nature and therefore more easy going, or less flexible and therefore more difficult. Difficult children tend to go against the grain of the household, resulting in a great deal of parental irritation.

9. Difficult children require more up front strategizing on the part of the parent. When you go to a backyard party with a flexible-style child, you don't have to do too much strategizing. Not so with the more difficult child. This style of child needs much greater clarification about what will happen if certain behaviors occur (e.g., "The last time we came over to your cousin's, you pushed the other children at the swings. I will be watching and if you push we will have to leave for about ten minutes until you are ready to come back to play.")

10. Don't be afraid of a little cool anger once in a while. The impact can be considerable and the message more in line with the reality of the moment (e.g., "I'm too angry to talk to you now," said in measured and direct tones.)

Final Words: Two Roads Diverged in a Yellow Wood

My personal and professional mission statement has always involved the question of how we can better help kids who are struggling, as well as assisting parents in their efforts with their children.

As I have pointed out, I believe that there are essentially two categories of children. In the first category are the kids who are pretty flexible in their style, getting along well with others and seeming to navigate the academic and social challenges of school. Their ride down the road is relatively smooth. These kids are engaged in a positive feedback loop that starts in the early grades and continues on throughout their school years and into college.

Then there is everyone else. Of this population, some kids are classified with learning disabilities, some have 504 plans, some are seen as not needing any services or accommodations yet are still struggling. These kids have a tough time of it because they may have trouble understanding social dynamics and seeing why they are not easily accepted by others. They may unwittingly be getting on people's nerves. Some children are easy targets for bullies. For them, school and social interactions are an ongoing struggle. The parents of these struggling children experience many different emotions, ranging from concern to utter frustration and, at times, anguish. Parents of these kids also feel a sense of helplessness.

I've been at this work long enough to be able to take a bird's eye view and see that so many kids that were struggling for any one reason or a host of reasons have turned out fine and are doing nicely in whatever direction they chose to go. I know this because many kids have contacted me to let me know that they have done well and are pursuing their own interests. I also run into parents who remind me of what a hard time it was when I was involved with them, but that things improved greatly over time.

I would like to believe that some of the improvements were due to the things that were said during our sessions or things that were tried, but this is hard to know with any real certainty. I have come to believe that some of the work done with kids and families is a form of seed planting, meaning that if the parent or child took a piece of advice and, in her own way tried it out, that some things do, in fact, take hold.

With all children, whether they are easy or difficult, I think we need to be calm, patient, and clear. We steer the ship where we want it to go. Captains of ships have to make tough decisions and set the course. Democracy among the deckhands and the captain will lead to a floundering ship going nowhere. On the other hand, if we exercise rigid control, the deckhands will look to mutiny in covert and overt ways. We need to find that middle position with kids—firm and clear, but not too definitive or rigid.

Societal changes are altering the landscape of childhood. Models that applied during another era are becoming obsolete. Sad as it may be that when you pass playgrounds or neighborhoods, you may not see too many kids out playing, that's the reality. Technology is altering all aspects of human interaction. There is no getting away from this. How many of us would readily part with our cell phones or agree to no longer have access to the Internet to go back to the way it was before these things existed in our world? My guess is not many, despite our complaining about how technology is changing us.

The only answer I come up with is to look to ourselves and set our own course with our children. If you value quiet time and think that you need electronic-free zones in your house, then set that as a parameter. If you want your child outside on a nice, sunny day, then start early and establish the rules. Do you want homework to go smoother? Then look to how homework is being conducted. You set the tone. You set the course. Even children who are "disabled" or "disordered," based on professional assessments, need clarity and direction from their adult leaders, perhaps even more so than others.

Always keep in mind that the formula of "you give and you get" is very basic, but far too many kids are not being held to that standard. They get without giving. They view playing video games as a right, not a privilege. There are very few rights. The rights of clothing, food, shelter, and parental protection are essential, but going on Facebook, playing Xbox, or driving a car are privileges. As the captains of the ship you need to determine whether your child has earned a privilege, or still needs to earn it.

Such messages are important for all children, but particularly for those struggling on the rougher road. Without clarity of message, these children have a hard time seeing the line, reading the signals, or judging cause and effect. They do not easily see their own part when things do not go well. Impulsive thinking leads to academic and social difficulty. Clarity and structure from parents who set the course is the ticket to help struggling children see situations better and make choices that work for them, not against them.

Listening to children, understanding them, and patiently seeing them as works in progress will help get you through some tough times. One expression I heard many years ago, spoken to parents who were concerned that their child was not measuring up or meeting expectations, summed it up. It went something like this: "Be patient. God isn't done with him yet." I think that was exactly on the money and it helped the parents to calm down and not be so focused on the immediate problems. It allowed the parents to gain some perspective.

So does the expression, "This, too, shall pass."

With virtually all child issues, remind yourself of this and things will look a lot brighter in the morning.

Appendix

Books

The following are very readable and practical books that are written for parents and professionals on a range of topics related to children:

The Big Book of Parenting Solutions: 101 Answers to Your Everyday Challenges and Wildest Worries by Michele Borba, Ed.D. (ISBN: 978-0-7879-8831-9)

What Your Explosive Child Is Trying to Tell You, by Douglas Riley, Ed.D. (ISBN: 978-0-618-70081-3)

Late, Lost & Unprepared: A Parent's Guide to Helping Children with Executive Functioning, by Joyce Cooper-Kahn, Ph.D. & Laurie Dietzel, Ph.D. (ISBN: 978-1-890627-84-3)

10 Days to a Less Defiant Child, by Jeffrey Bernstein, Ph.D. (ISBN: 978-1-56924-301-5)

No More Misbehavin': 38 Difficult Behaviors and How to Stop Them, by Michele Borba, Ed.D. (ISBN: 07879-6617-7)

The Family ADHD Solution by Mark Bertin, M.D., (ISBN: 978-0-230-10505-8)

Delivered from Distraction: Getting the Most Out of Life with Attention Deficit Disorder, by Edward M. Hallowell, M.D. & John Ratey, M.D. (ISBN: 978-0-345-44231)

Teacher's Guide to ADHD by Robert Reid & Joseph Johnson (ISBN: 1-60918-979-2)

No One to Play With: The Social Side of Learning Disabilities, revised edition by Betty B. Osman, Ed.D. (ISBN:

Taking Charge of ADHD: The Complete, Authoritative Guide for Parents (Revised Edition) by Russell A. Barkley PhD (ISBN-10: 1572305606)

The Kazdin Method for Parenting the Defiant Child, by Alan E. Kazdin, Ph.D. (ISBN: 978-0-547-08582-1)

No More Meltdowns, by Jed Baker, Ph.D. (ISBN: 978-1-932565-62-1)

Help Your Child or Teen Get Back on Track by Kenneth H. Tallan, M.D. (ISBN: 978-1-84310-3)

The Everything Parent's Guide to Children With Dyslexia by Abigail Marshall (ISBN: 978-1-59337-135-7)

Straight Talk About Psychiatric Medications for Kids by Timothy E. Wilens, M.D. (ISBN: 978-1-59385-842-1)

The Explosive Child: A New Approach for Understanding and Parenting Easily Frustrated, Chronically Inflexible Children, by Ross Greene Ph.D. (ISBN-10: 0061906190)

It's So Much Work to Be Your Friend by Richard Lavoie (ISBN: 978-07432-5465-6)

The Misunderstood Child: Understanding & Coping With Your Child's Learning Disabilities by Larry B. Silver, M.D. (ISBN: 0-307-33863-0)

Overcoming Dyslexia: A New and Complete Science-Based Program for Reading Problems at Any Level, Sally Shaywitz, M.D. (ISBN-10: 0679781595)

Smart but Scattered by Peg Dawson, Ed.D. Y Richard Guare, Ph.D. (ISBN: 978-1-59385-445-4)

The Mouse in the Microwave by John Kellmayer, Ed.D. (ISBN-10: 0615563627)

Reading Disabilities: Beating the Odds, Howard Margolis, Ed.D. & Gary Brannigan, Ph.D. (ISBN-10: 0615279007)

Writing Skills (Books 1 & 2) by Diana Hanbury King (ISBN-10: 0838820506)

The Shut-Down Learner: Helping Your Academically Discouraged Child by Richard Selznick, PhD (ISBN: 978-1-59181-078-0)

Organizations and Websites

The following are great organizations with informative and helpful websites:

- National Center for Learning Disabilities (NCLD): www.ncld.org
- LD OnLine.org: www.ldonline.org
- Learning Disabilities Association of America (LDA): www.ldanatl.org
- ADDitue: Living Well With Attention Deficit: www.additudemag.com
- Great Schools: www.greatschools.org
- CHADD: (Children & Adults With Attention Deficit/Hyperactivity Disorder): www.chadd.org
- Reading Rockets: www.readingrockets.org
- International Dyslexia Association: www.interdys.org
- Eunice Kennedy Shriver National Institute of Child Health & Human Development (NICHD): www.nichd.nih.gov

About the Author

Photo: Patrick Flanigan

Dr. Richard Selznick ("Dr. Selz") is a psychologist, nationally certified school psychologist, adjunct graduate school professor, and assistant professor of pediatrics. As the director of the Cooper Learning Center, he oversees a program that assesses and treats a broad range of learning and school-based behavioral problems in children. The Cooper Learning Center is a Division of the Children's Regional Hospital of Cooper University Hospital. Dr. Selznick is also the author of *The Shut-Down Learner: Helping Your Academically Discouraged Child.*

Dr. Selznick speaks to parents and educators on a variety of topics related to school struggling. A down-to-earth presenter who discusses difficult topics without using jargon, he has presented to educators in Dubai and Abu Dhabi as well as throughout the United States. A native of Staten Island, New York, Dr. Selznick lives in Haddonfield, New Jersey.

He can be reached by email at contact@drselz.com. For more information, please see www.drselz.com, Facebook (Find Shut Down Learner), and Twitter @DrSelz.

Sentient Publications, LLC publishes books on cultural creativity, experimental education, transformative spirituality, holistic health, new science, ecology, and other topics, approached from an integral viewpoint. Our authors are intensely interested in exploring the nature of life from fresh perspectives, addressing life's great questions, and fostering the full expression of the human potential. Sentient Publications' books arise from the spirit of inquiry and the richness of the inherent dialogue between writer and reader.

Our Culture Tools series is designed to give social catalyzers and cultural entrepreneurs the essential information, technology, and inspiration to forge a sustainable, creative, and compassionate world.

We are very interested in hearing from our readers. To direct suggestions or comments to us, or to be added to our mailing list, please contact:

SENTIENT PUBLICATIONS, LLC

1113 Spruce Street
Boulder, CO 80302
303-443-2188
contact@sentientpublications.com
www.sentientpublications.com